# Targum Americana

## The Bible Understood

## VaYikra - Leviticus

By

Irwin (Yirmi) Tyler

Ahl Kayn Publications
Spring Valley, NY

# TABLE OF CONTENTS

i

## INTERPRETER'S COMMENTS

Why was this interpretation of the Word of God created? The answer really is very simple. Those of us who did not grow up with Biblical Hebrew, the Holy Language, as a living language find it very difficult to appreciate the nuances and poetry in the words of Torah. This lack of fluency in the language causes confusion for many. Too, the great Jewish teachers and commentators, who were very well versed in the language, often disagreed as to their understanding of God's meaning, or they expanded the thoughts of those who commented before them. This again resulted in apparently conflicting translations and commentaries.

More than that, even the simple meaning of these Hebrew words is not always easily understood by even those who have studied the language. The reason, again, is very simple. God placed within His Words of Torah many levels of meaning, for us to extract as the times dictate. This often leaves us bewildered, wondering what we are learning from the Torah. Thus, this book.

In some ways, this work follows in the tradition of Targum Onkelos, written for the Aramaic-speaking Jewish world of the Second Temple period. But this is not really a definitive English translation, nor a complete explanation of the written Torah. It is an attempt to bring together thoughts and commentaries of many of our Sages so as to make sense of what often is language strange to our ears. At the same time, it is incomplete. Hints, alternative explanations, historical discoveries each bring new understandings and levels of understandings. That being the case, this work is incomplete, merely a starting point for understanding God's Word.

## INTERPRETER'S COMMENTS

What are shown in this work as quoted statements are meant to offer the sense, not the direct words of the speaker. It is, if my skill has been applied well, a readable, consistent, understandable presentation of every single *posuk* (sentence) in the Torah based on one or more readings of the revered commentators who have maintained and clarified the stream of understanding starting with the teaching of the Torah by Moses (Moshe) at Mt. Sinai. Where comments differ greatly I have selected either one that made the most sense to me within the simple context of the actual Torah text, or I merged ideas in a way that made sense to me. In either case, I tried as much as possible to make the language easily understood while allowing the English language to "speak" to you in its own unique majestic manner.

## INTERPRETER'S COMMENTS

I have also chosen to transliterate names (Chava/Eve) and terms (tzaraas/leprosy) where the names or terms in the Hebrew have an important meaning in themselves and common English usage in other Biblical translations clearly are inaccurate or misleading.

As understandable as it may be, this work is no substitute for the many commentaries in a variety of languages that have sought to tease out the countless levels of meaning merely hinted at here.

I pray that God has given me the wisdom to select properly and to present clearly. I pray that in the words I have chosen, I have not introduced unintended or confusing ideas. I pray that God gives to you the ability to receive through my words the love of the Words of His Torah and creates in you the want to probe ever more deeply into its teachings.


Yirmi Tyler    2011 - 5772

# THE NAMES OF GOD

We name things to identify them to others and to provide a shortcut to knowing "all" about them. When we say a lion is a cat we automatically know many of its characteristics because it is a cat. At the same time, we know special characteristics about the creature we call "lion" over and above its being a cat. We can talk about a lion to someone who, with this knowledge of the name "lion" and the name "cat", can immediately bring to mind an understanding of this creature with a great deal of detail even though few, if any, words of description were spoken.

But, God is different. He has no category. He has no bodily nature. He can't be seen. There is nothing that can be compared to Him from which to draw out a description of God. All English translations call God "God". There is no other name in English that works. Thus, the English word "God" is totally inadequate, for it tells us nothing about God.

The original Hebrew, the Holy Tongue, has many different words, names and phrases that refer to God. In English they are all translated, "God". Thus, anyone reading an English translation of the Bible will lose significant understanding. God's actions when He is making Himself known as "Creator and Ruler" are understood very differently from when He is making Himself known as "Source of Mercy", even though His actions may be the same in each case.

In order to overcome this limitation of the English language, each time a name/descriptive term of God changes in this Targum, I explain how, in that instance, a specific, limited characteristic of God's nature is being exhibited. Every subsequent name "God" holds that understanding until there is a change and a new explanation is presented. And because the name "God" may extend several pages unchanged in the Hebrew, I place a reminder at the top of each page of the most recently presented explanation of God's name.

For example:

## BERESHIT / GENESIS – <u>VAYERA</u>

*(in His nature as the Only God, the Creator of all existence)*

**20**-17 ~ Avraham prayed to God, the God whom he knew was in His nature as the Only God, the Creator of all existence. Then God (in His nature as Creator and Ruler) healed Avimelech and his wife and slave girls, so that they would be able to have children. **20**-18 ~ For God (in His nature as Source of Mercy) had stopped all childbearing in Avimelech's house because of Avraham's wife Sarah.

**21**-1 ~ When the time came that God had told Sarah would come, God did for her as He had promised. **21**-2 ~ Sarah became pregnant, and she gave birth to Avraham's son, even as old as he was. It was exactly at the time that God (in His nature as Creator and Ruler) had promised to him. **21**-3 ~ Avraham gave the name Yitzchak to his son whom Sarah had borne, this name noting his unusual birth, for the name means "he will laugh". **21**-4 ~ Avraham circumcised his son Yitzchak when he was eight days old, just as God had commanded him.

## SOURCES FOR THE INTERPRETATIONS

*These commentaries and Biblical translations were themselves the products of their author's own insights arising from centuries of transmitted wisdom from Rambam, Ramban, Ibn Ezra, Sforno, Malbim, Saadiah Gaon, Vilna Gaon, Abarbanel, and hundreds of other sages and teachers of Torah, filling thousands of volumes.*

Chumash – The Gutnick Edition – With Rashi's Commentary, Targum Onkelos, Haftoras and Commentary anthologized from Classic Rabbinic Texts and the works of the Lubavitcher Rebbe
      Compiled and Adapted by Rabbi Chaim Miller
      Published and Distributed by Kol Menachem

Pentateuch and Haftorahs
      Edited by Dr. J. H. Hertz    The Soncino Press
          Hebrew Text, English Translation and Commentary

The Call of the Torah
      Rabbi Elie Munk     Art Scroll Mesorah Series
         An anthology of interpretation and commentary on the Five Books of Moses

The Chumash The Stone Edition    The Art Scroll Series –
                        Mesorah Publications, Ltd
      Rabbi Nosson Scherman/Rabbi Meir Zlotowitz,
      General Editors

The Living Torah
> Rabbi Aryeh Kaplan   Maznaim Publishing Corporation
> A new translation based on traditional Jewish
> sources

The Pentateuch – Translation and Commentary
> Rabbi Samson Raphael Hirsch   Judaica Press, Ltd
> English translation by Yitzchak Levy

The Pentateuch and Rashi's Commentary – A Linear Translation into
> English
> Rabbi Abraham ben Isaiah and Rabbi Benjamin Sharfman in
> collaboration with Dr. Harry M. Orlinsky and Rabbi Dr. Morris
> Charner
> S. S. & R. Publishing Company, Inc.

The Torah Anthology – MeAm Loez
> Rabbi Yaakov Culi   Moznaim Publishing Company
> Translated by Rabbi Aryeh Kaplan

*The result in this Targum is that it may combine more than one commentary within the same sentence, woven together in a way that removes what would otherwise appear as contradictions.*

## VAYIKRA / LEVITICUS – <u>VAYIKRA</u>
## Understanding this Holy Book

**<u>Targum Americana,</u>** as much as is possible in English, maintains the majesty of the Holy language of the Torah. It is not a translation but an interpretation, verse by verse, based on over 2,000 years of understandings offered by its original interpreters and the great later Jewish Sages and commentators.

**Study of this work is not a substitute for learning Torah in the original Holy Language. Learning Torah without the clarifications of the Sages and commentators surely will lead to gross errors in understanding.**

**VAYIKRA 1**-1 ~ Since Moshe could not come into the Communion Tent while the cloud rested on it, God in His nature as Source of Mercy called to Moshe from the Communion Tent, saying to him, **1**-2 ~ "Speak to the Yisra'elites and tell them the following: 'When you bring an animal as an offering to God, this sacrifice may be only from among these mammals: cattle, sheep or goats.

**1**-3 ~ 'If the sacrifice is a cattle offering, meant to be a burnt offering, a sacrifice that is completely burned, it must be an unblemished male. One must bring it of his own free will to the entrance of the Communion Tent as an offering before God. **1**-4 ~ He shall press his hands heavily on the head of the animal, and it shall then be accepted as an atonement for him.

**1**-5 ~ 'The young bull shall be slaughtered in the proper manner before God inside the enclosure of the Tabernacle. Aharon's sons, the priests, shall then bring forward the blood which was collected during the slaughter. The blood shall be splashed on all sides of the altar that is in front of the entrance to the Communion Tent.

**1**-6 ~ 'When the burnt offering has been slaughtered it shall be skinned and cut into pieces. **1**-7 ~ Aharon's sons shall place fire on the altar, then add wood to the fire. **1**-8 ~ Aharon's sons shall then arrange on top of the burning wood the cut pieces of the offering, the head, and the fatty intestinal membranes and those organs as they will have been taught to identify. **1**-9 ~ The intestines and the legs must first be scrubbed clean with water before being placed on the fire. The priest, one of Aharon's sons, shall thus direct and assure the proper burning of the animal on the altar as a completely burned fire offering, creating a pleasing fragrance to God.

# VAYIKRA / LEVITICUS – VAYIKRA

*(in His nature as Source of Mercy)*

1-10 ~ 'If one's burnt offering is a smaller animal, it shall be taken from the sheep or goats. One must, like with the bull, present an unblemished male. 1-11 ~ He shall have it slaughtered before God on the north side of the altar, opposite the altar's ramp. The priests, who are Aharon's descendants, shall dash its blood on all sides of the altar.

1-12 ~ 'The animal shall be cut into pieces. The priest shall then arrange these, along with the head and the intestinal membrane, upon the fire on the altar. 1-13 ~ But first, the internal organs and the feet shall be washed with water. The priest shall then complete the offering by burning every-thing upon the altar. It is a complete burnt offering, creating a pleasing fragrance to God.

1-14 ~ 'If one's burnt offering is a bird, he may bring a turtle dove or a young common dove whose feathers have not yet begun to glisten. 1-15 ~ The priest shall bring the bird to the altar and, with the fingernail of his thumb, drive it through the back of the bird's neck and sever the spine, the windpipe and the gullet. After draining the bird's blood on the upper half of the altar's south-east corner, he shall sever the head and burn it on the altar.

1-16 ~ 'He shall remove the bird's crop, entrails and the feathers surround-ing this area and cast them onto the pile of ashes that had been collected and placed to the east of the altar that morning.

# VAYIKRA / LEVITICUS – VAYIKRA

*(in His nature as Source of Mercy)*

**1**-17 ~ 'He shall partially split the bird apart by its wings, being careful not to separate the parts. The priest shall then burn it upon the wood fire on the altar. It is a burnt offering, a fire offering that creates a pleasing fragrance to God.

**2**-1 ~ 'If a person presents a meal offering *(a mincha offering)* to God, his offering must consist of the finest quality wheat, one-tenth ephah *(2 quarts)* coarsely ground and sifted. On it he must pour a log *(10 ounces)* of olive oil and a handful of frankincense. **2**-2 ~ He shall bring it to Aharon, or to the priests who are Aharon's descendants in his day. A priest shall then scoop out with the three middle fingers of one hand an amount no less than the volume of two olives. The priest shall remove the frankincense, then separately burn this wheat portion and the frankincense on the altar as a remembrance fire offering, creating a pleasing fragrance to God. **2**-3 ~ The rest of the meal offering shall belong to the priests. It is a holy of holies among the fire offerings to God.

**2**-4 ~ 'If a person presents a meal offering that was baked in an oven, it may consist either of ten unleavened loaves *(chalah)* made from one-tenth ephah of coarsely ground wheat meal kneaded together with olive oil and warm water, or one-tenth ephah of coarsely ground wheat meal made into ten flat wafers *(matzot)*, with a log of olive oil rubbed well into the surface of each matzah.

# VAYIKRA / LEVITICUS – VAYIKRA

*(in His nature as Source of Mercy)*

**2-5** ~ 'If the sacrifice is a pan fried offering, made from one-tenth ephah of coarsely ground wheat meal mixed with olive oil and then kneaded together with warm water, it shall be fried quickly in olive oil before it has become leavened.

**2-6** ~ 'All these baked or fried meal offerings first shall be broken into olive-sized pieces. Olive oil shall be poured upon the pieces and these will then be burned upon the altar.

**2-7** ~ 'If your sacrifice is a meal offering prepared in a deep pot, olive oil shall be placed into the pot and then whole wheat meal placed into the oil.

**2-8** ~ 'These are the ways you may prepare any of your meal offerings to God. These shall be presented to the priest, who will bring it to the altar. **2-9** ~ The priest shall then lift out a memorial portion from the meal offering and elevate it by burning it on the altar. It is a fire offering, creating a pleasing fragrance to God. **2-10** ~ The remainder of the meal offering then belongs to Aharon and his descendants. This is one of God's fire offerings, a holy of holies.

**2-11** ~ 'Do not make out of leavened dough any meal offering to God, for you may not burn any fire offering sacrifice that is leavened, nor that is sweetened. **2-12** ~ Although these may be brought as a first-fruit offering to God, they are not to be brought up to the altar as a pleasing fragrance to God. **2-13** ~ Moreover, you must salt every meal offering before their being placed on the altar. Do not leave out this salt for the meal offering;

*(in His nature as Source of Mercy)*

this salt represents your covenant with God.  Moreover, you must also offer salt with your animal sacrifices.

**2-14** ~ 'When you bring an offering of the first grain, the *omer* offering, it should be harvested as soon as it ripens on the stalk.  Your first grain offering shall consist of fresh kernels of your best grade of barley, roasted in a perforated pan, and then ground into coarse meal.  **2-15** ~ Place olive oil and frankincense on it, just as you would for any other meal offering.

**2-16** ~ 'Since this is a fire offering to God, the priest shall take a memorial portion from the coarse meal, oil, and frankincense and burn these on the altar.

**3-1** ~ 'If one brings before God a peace offering that is from cattle, the offering may be either an unblemished male or an unblemished female.

**3-2** ~ 'He shall press his hands heavily on the head of the animal, and it shall then be slaughtered at the entrance of the Communion Tent.  The priests, Aharon's descendants, shall dash its blood on all sides of the altar.

**3-3** ~ 'The portion of the peace offerings that are presented as a fire offering to God must include the layer of fat covering all four stomach compartments.  **3-4** ~ Also to be removed for burning are the two kidneys along with the fat on them, the fat attached to the maw and to the spleen, the fat where the hind legs extend into the body cavity, the fat on the lobe of the liver next to the kidneys, and the diaphragm.

# VAYIKRA / LEVITICUS – VAYIKRA

*(in His nature as Source of Mercy)*

**3-5** ~ 'The priests, Aharon's descendants, shall burn these on the altar, along with the burnt offering that may still be burning on the altar. This is a fire offering, creating a pleasing fragrance to God.

**3-6** ~ 'If one's sacrifice of a peace offering to God is taken from the smaller animals this must be an unblemished animal, whether it be male or female. **3-7** ~ If his sacrifice is a sheep he shall present it before God **3-8** ~ to be slaughtered in front of the Communion Tent. He shall press his hands heavily on the head of the animal, and it shall then be slaughtered there. The priests, Aharon's descendants, shall dash its blood on all sides of the altar.

**3-9** ~ 'From the sacrifice of a smaller animal as a peace offering, a fire offering to to God, he shall separate out and remove the following: the fat with the whole of the rump and tail towards the backbone, all the fat that covers or is attached to the stomachs, **3-10** ~ the two kidneys and the fat that is on them along the flanks, and the lobe over the liver near the kidneys.

**3-11** ~ 'The priest shall burn them on the altar to be consumed as a fire offering to God.

**3-12** ~ 'If one's sacrifice of a peace offering to God is a goat **3-13** ~ he shall press his hands heavily upon its head, and it shall then be slaughtered at the entrance of the Communion Tent. The priests, Aharon's descendants, shall then dash its blood on all sides of the altar.

# VAYIKRA / LEVITICUS – VAYIKRA

*(in His nature as Source of Mercy)*

**3-14** ~ 'As his fire offering sacrifice to God, he shall present the layers of fat that cover the stomachs, and all the other fat attached to the stomachs. **3-15** ~ Also to be removed are the two kidneys along with the fat on them along the flanks, and the lobe over the liver near the kidneys. **3-16** ~ The priests shall burn them on the altar to be consumed as a fire offering to God, creating a pleasing fragrance to God.

'All the fats which have been described are not for you, they belong to God. **3-17** ~ You and all your descendants have been given this law for all time, wherever you may live, that you may not eat any fat of these animals that is meant to be sacrificed. Nor, too, may you consume their blood.'"

**4-1** ~ God spoke to Moshe, giving him these words of law to instruct the people:

**4-2** ~ "This is the law concerning a person who commits a sin accidentally by violating any of those prohibitions specified by God for which the penalty is being "spiritually cut off" *(karet)*.

**4-3** ~ "Firstly, if the anointed High Priest, Aharon's descendant, inadvertently violates the law, thereby bringing guilt to his people, he shall bring an unblemished bull in its second year as a sacrifice, a sin offering to God for this violation. **4-4** ~ He shall bring the bull before God, to the entrance of the Communion Tent, where he shall press his hands heavily

*(in His nature as Source of Mercy)*

upon its head, and it shall then be slaughtered in the prescribed manner.

**4-5** ~ "The anointed priest shall bring the bull's blood into the Communion Tent, the enclosure of the Tabernacle. **4-6** ~ The priest shall dip his finger into the blood and sprinkle it seven times before God, toward the cloth partition in the Sanctuary, being careful that the blood not touch the partition. **4-7** ~ The priest shall then place some of the blood on the incense altar which is before God, in the Communion Tent. The rest of the blood he shall spill out at the base of the sacrificial altar, which is in front of the Communion Tent at its entrance.

**4-8** ~ "He shall remove all the fat that covers or is attached to the stomachs, **4-9** ~ the two kidneys and the fat that is on them along the flanks, and the lobe over the liver near the kidneys, **4-10** ~ these being the same as he is to do with the peace offering. He shall then burn them on the sacrificial altar.

**4-11** ~ "He shall take the bull's skin, every bit of its flesh, and whatever food is found in its intestines **4-12** ~ and he shall bring all of this to the same ritually pure place outside the camp where the altar's ashes are deposited. The bull's parts shall be spread out upon wood which has been placed upon the ashes and set aflame.

**4-13** ~ "If the entire community commits an inadvertent sin, this being a result of the truth being unknown by the Sanhedrin or the congregation,

# VAYIKRA / LEVITICUS – VAYIKRA

*(in His nature as Source of Mercy)*

and it is one of the specified "you shall not" prohibitory commandments of God, the guilt shall be upon the community as a whole.  4-14 ~ When the violation becomes known the congregation must bring a young bull as a sin offering and present it before the Communion Tent.

4-15 ~ "Before God, the members of the Sanhedrin or three community elders shall press their hands heavily on the head of the animal and it shall then be slaughtered.  4-16 ~ The anointed priest shall bring some of the bull's blood into the Communion Tent,  4-17 ~ where he shall dip his fingers into the blood and sprinkle the blood seven times before God toward the cloth partition, being careful that the blood not touch the partition. 4-18 ~ He shall then place some of the blood on each of the horn-shaped projections of the incense altar that is before God in the Communion Tent. The rest of the blood he shall spill out at the base of the sacrificial altar which is in front of the Communion Tent's entrance.

4-19 ~ "He shall then separate out all of its fat, which shall be burned on the altar,  4-20 ~ doing the same with this bull as he did with the bull of the sin offering for the anointed priest. The priest shall thus make atonement for the community so that they shall be forgiven.

4-21 ~ "As he did with that first bull, he shall remove this bull to a place outside the camp and burn it.  This is the sin offering for the entire congregation.

# VAYIKRA / LEVITICUS – VAYIKRA

*(in His nature as Source of Mercy)*

4-22 ~ "If the leader of the Yisra'elites commits a sin by inadvertently violating one of God's commands that he has been told not to do, he incurs guilt for which he must make atonement.    4-23 ~ When he is made aware of the sin that he has committed, he must bring an unblemished male goat in its first year as his sacrifice.  4-24 ~ He shall press his hands heavily upon its head, and it shall then be slaughtered before God as a sin offering on the north side of the altar, opposite the altar's ramp, in the same place as the burnt offering was slaughtered.

4-25 ~ "With his finger the priest shall then place some of the blood of the sin offering on each of the horn-shaped projections of the sacrificial altar.  The rest of the blood he shall spill out at the base of the sacrificial altar, which is in front of the Communion Tent at its entrance.

4-26 ~ "All the animal's fat shall be burned on the altar, just like the fat of the peace offerings.  In this way the priest shall complete the process of atonement for the leader, and he will be forgiven,

4-27 ~ "'There are certain commandments of God you will learn of which He has prohibited to be done. If an ordinary Yisra'elite commits an inadvertent violation of any of these, he is considered guilty.  4-28 ~ When he becomes aware of this violation he must offer an unblemished female goat to atone for the sin he has committed.  4-29 ~ He shall press his hands heavily on the head of the animal, and then he shall have this sin offering slaughtered on the north side of the altar, in the same place as the burnt offering.

# VAYIKRA / LEVITICUS – VAYIKRA

*(in His nature as Source of Mercy)*

4-30 ~ "The priest shall take some of the goat's blood with his fingers and place it on the each of horn-shaped projections of the sacrificial altar. He shall then spill out the rest of the blood at the altar's base. 4-31 ~ Just as he did with the fat of the peace offering, the priest shall remove all of the fat of the goat and burn it on the altar, creating a pleasing fragrance to God. In this way the priest shall make atonement for that Yisra'elite, and he will be forgiven.

4-32 ~ "If he brings a sheep as a sin offering it shall be an unblemished female. 4-33 ~ He shall press his hands heavily on the head of the animal, and then he shall have this sin offering slaughtered on the north side of the altar, in the same placed as the burnt offering.

4-34 ~ "The priest shall take some of the sheep's blood with his fingers and place it on each of the horn-shaped projections of the sacrificial altar. He shall then spill out the rest of the blood at the altar's base. 4-35 ~ He shall remove all its choice parts, these being the fat with the whole of the rump and tail towards the backbone, all the fat that covers or is attached to the stomachs, the two kidneys and the fat that is on them along the flanks, and the lobe over the liver near the kidneys, just as he removed these choice parts of the sheep brought as a peace offering. He shall burn these parts on the altar along with the fire offerings dedicated to God. The priest will thus make atonement for the sin that the person committed, and he will be forgiven.

## VAYIKRA / LEVITICUS – VAYIKRA

*(in His nature as Source of Mercy)*

**5**-1 ~ "This is the law concerning a person who sins in any of the following ways:

"If he is bound by an oath to give evidence in court, where he was a witness who saw or knew something, should he not testify he must bear guilt for this.

**5**-2 ~ "It may happen that a person may touch an animal that is ritually unclean, whether it is a dead wild animal or a dead domestic non-kosher animal, or any dead unclean creeping animal *(a sheretz)*. The person thereby becomes ritually unclean. While in this ritually unclean state he may forget and eat of something sanctified, meaning it is holy, or he may go into a sanctified area. The person shall bear the guilt of this sin. **5**-3 ~ Likewise, he shall bear his guilt for a violation that he eventually remembers when he had become ritually unclean for having come in contact with something itself ritually unclean because of a human being.

**5**-4 ~ "Also, a person is guilty if he makes a verbal oath to do something, whether it is for good or for bad, even if it is about something that has already happened, and he forgot about it and then violated this oath.

"In any of these cases, the person is considered guilty as soon as he realizes what he has done.

**5**-5 ~ "When he is guilty in any of these cases he must confess the sin that

# VAYIKRA / LEVITICUS – VAYIKRA

*(in His nature as Source of Mercy)*

he has committed. **5-6** ~ He must also bring a guilt *(asham)* offering to God for the sin he has committed. This sin offering must be a female sheep or goat. The priest will then make atonement for the person's sin.

**5-7** ~ 'If he can not afford a sheep or goat, the guilt offering that he presents to God for his sin shall be two turtle doves or two young common doves. One shall be a sin offering and the other shall be a burnt offering. **5-8** ~ He shall bring them to the priest, who shall first sacrifice the one for the sin offering. The priest shall drive the fingernail of his thumb through the back of the bird's neck and sever the spine, windpipe and the gullet, but without separating the head from the body. **5-9** ~ He shall them drain the blood on the side of the altar. The rest of the blood of the sin offering shall be drained at the altar's base.

**5-10** ~ "When the sin offering is completed he shall sacrifice the second bird as he has been instructed in the law of the burnt offering. In this way the priest shall make atonement for the sin that the person has committed, and he will be forgiven.

**5-11** ~ "If he can not afford the two turtle doves or two common doves for his sin, in their place he must bring one-tenth ephah of wheat meal as his sin offering. Because it is a sin offering he shall not place any oil or frank-incense on it. **5-12**~ He shall bring it to the priest, and the priest shall scoop up three fingers full of the wheat meal as a

*(in His nature as Source of Mercy)*

memorial portion.  This portion the priest shall burn on the altar as the person's sin offering, along with God's other fire offerings.

5-13 ~ "The priest shall thus make atonement for the person's sin with one of these sin offerings.  The unburnt portion of the sin offering shall belong to the priest."

5-14 ~ God spoke to Moshe saying:

5-15 ~ "If a person sins inadvertently by taking for his personal use something that has been set aside for God, he shall bring his guilt offering to God.   It shall consist of an unblemished ram in its second year, having a value of two shekels according to the value of the Temple shekel.  This is to be offered as a guilt *(asham)* offering.

5-16 ~ "If he takes for his personal use something that has been set aside for God, he must make full restitution, adding one fifth to it and giving it to the priest. With this and the guilt offering ram, the priest shall make atonement for him, and he shall be forgiven.

5-17 ~ "If a person believes he may have sinned by violating any of those prohibitions specified by God for which the penalty is being "spiritually cut off" *(karet)*, although he is unsure that he did indeed sin, still it is considered as if he had sinned toward God and he bears responsibility for the sin.  5-18 ~ He must bring an unblemished ram in its second year as his

*(in His nature as Source of Mercy)*

guilt offering. It must have a value of two shekels according to the value of the Temple shekel. The priest shall then make atonement for this inadvertent sin committed without definite knowledge, and he shall be forgiven. **5**-19 ~ A person is required to bring a guilt offering for this sin toward God."

**5**-20 ~ God spoke to Moshe saying:

**5**-21 ~ "This is the law concerning a person who sins by committing a sin against God by lying to his neighbor concerning such activities as: damage to or improper use of the other person's property, or about details of a loan or business deal, or about a robbery, or withholding money due, or any illegal monetary cheating, **5**-22 ~ or finding an object and denying it. If the person swears falsely concerning such acts of human relations, he is considered to have sinned.

**5**-23 ~ "When he becomes aware that he is guilty of such a sin he must return the stolen article, the withheld funds, the article left for safekeeping, the found article, **5**-24 ~ or anything of a like nature about which he swore falsely. On the day he brings his guilt sacrifice he must make restitution of the item to the rightful owner and then add one fifth to it of the value the item had on the day of his sin.

**5**-25 ~ "After making restitution he must bring to the priest his sin offering to God. This is a guilt offering, which shall be an unblemished ram worth

# VAYIKRA / LEVITICUS – VAYIKRA

*(in His nature as Source of Mercy)*

the amount prescribed by the priest. **5-26** ~ The priest shall then make atonement for him before God, and he shall be forgiven for any such crime he had committed."

## VAYIKRA / LEVITICUS – <u>TZAV</u>
### Understanding this Holy Book

**<u>Targum Americana,</u>** as much as is possible in English, maintains the majesty of the Holy language of the Torah. It is not a translation but an interpretation, verse by verse, based on over 2,000 years of understandings offered by its original interpreters and the great later Jewish Sages and commentators.

Study of this work is not a substitute for learning Torah in the original Holy Language. Learning Torah without the clarifications of the Sages and commentators surely will lead to gross errors in understanding.

## VAYIKRA / LEVITICUS – TZAV

*(in His nature as Source of Mercy)*

**6**-1 ~ God spoke to Moshe, telling him   **6**-2 ~ to relate the following instructions to Aharon and to his descendants:

"This is the law of the burnt offering. This offering shall remain burning on the altar all night until the morning so that the fire of the incense alter may be ignited with it.  **6**-3 ~ The priest shall then put on his linen vestments, including his linen pants. With a shovel he shall remove the ashes of the burnt offerings from the fire on the altar and place the ashes to the southeast near the ramp of the altar.

**6**-4 ~ "He shall then remove his linen vestments and clothe himself in garments of lesser quality.  Now he shall take the ashes to a ritually clean place outside the camp.

**6**-5 ~ "Each morning the fire of the altar shall be ignited with the burning remains of the previous day's offerings.  The priest shall add new wood to kindle the fire.  On this wood he shall arrange burnt offerings, and here he shall burn the choice parts of the peace offerings.  **6**-6 ~ In this way a constant fire shall be kept burning on the altar; it shall not be allowed to burn out.

**6**-7 ~ "This is the law of the meal offering: One of Aharon's descendants, shall offer it before God near the altar at its south-west corner.  **6**-8 ~ With his three middle fingers of one hand

*(in His nature as Source of Mercy)*

he shall lift up some of this offering's wheat meal and oil mixture, including the frankincense, and he shall burn both the meal and frankincense on the altar, creating a pleasing fragrance to God. This is the memorial portion to God.

**6-9** ~ "Aharon and his descendants shall then eat the rest of the offering, in the form of unleavened bread, in a holy place, this being the enclosure of the Communion Tent. **6-10** ~ Be careful that this offering does not become baked into leavened bread.

"I have given this portion of the offering to Aharon and his descendants as their portion of My fire offerings. It is a holy of holies, like the sin offering and the guilt offering. **6-11** ~ Every male among Aharon's descendants may eat it. It is an eternal law for all generations that this portion be separated out from God's fire offerings. Any food touching this meal offering will absorb some of the taste of the meal offering, thereby becoming holy as well."

**6-12** ~ God spoke to Moshe these words: **6-13** ~ "The following offering must be brought by Aharon and his descendants on the day he is anointed as High Priest. It shall consist of one-tenth ephah of wheat meal. It shall be like a daily meal offering, with one half offered in the morning and one-half in the evening. **6-14** ~ It shall be mixed well with three logs *(almost one*

*(in His nature as Source of Mercy)*

quart) of olive oil and divided into twelve parts. Each is to be quickly boiled then lightly baked into wafers.

"The wafers then shall be fried in olive oil on a flat pan and presented as an offering, a pleasing fragrance to God. **6-15** ~ It is a law for all time that the High Priest, Aharon and his descendants, shall prepare and offer it. **6-16** ~ It must be completely burned and not eaten, in the same way as are all meal offerings brought by a priest."

**6-17** ~ God told Moshe **6-18** ~ to relate the following message to Aharon and his descendants: "This is the law of the slaughter of the sin offering. The sin offering must be slaughtered before God in the same place that the burnt offering is slaughtered. It is holy of holies.

**6-19** ~ "Any priest fit to offer it may eat it. It must be eaten in a holy place within the enclosure of the Communion Tent.

**6-20** ~ "Any ordinary food touching a sin offering will absorb some of it's taste, thereby changing the ordinary food into a holy food.

"Should the blood of a sin offering splash onto any garment, that garment must be washed clean in a sanctified area.

# VAYIKRA / LEVITICUS – TZAV

*(in His nature as Source of Mercy)*

**6-21** ~ Any clay pot in which a sin offering has been cooked may no longer be used; it must be broken. However, should a sin offering have been cooked in a copper vessel the vessel may be purged in boiling water and then rinsed with water.

**6-22** ~ "Although the sin offering is a holy of holies, any male priest may eat it. **6-23** ~ Any sin offering whose blood has been brought into the Communion Tent to make atonement in the Sanctuary may not be eaten. It must be burned in fire.

**7-1** ~ "This is the law of the guilt, offering, which is a holy of holies. **7-2** ~ The guilt offering must be slaughtered in the same place that the burnt offering is slaughtered. It's blood must be dashed on all sides of the altar. **7-3** ~ All the choice parts must be removed and presented, these being the fat with the whole of the rump and tail towards the backbone, all the fat that covers or is attached to the stomachs, **7-4** ~ the two kidneys and the fat that is on them along the flanks, and the lobe over the liver near the kidneys. **7-5** ~ The priest must burn all of these on the alter as a guilt offering, a fire offering to God.

**7-6** ~ "What is not set aside to be burned may be eaten by the priests, Aharon and his descendants. These must be eaten only in a

*(in His nature as Source of Mercy)*

sanctified area, for these are holy of holies. **7-7** ~ The sin offering and the guilt offering have exactly the same laws insofar as their unburned parts can be given only to priests fit to offer them. **7-8** ~ Any priest who is fit to sacrifice a person's burnt offering may share in that animal's skin after the offering has been burnt.

**7-9** ~ "The remaining portion of any meal offering, whether baked in an oven, pan fried, or deep fried may be shared by any priest who is fit to sacrifice that offering. **7-10** ~ A meal offering, whether mixed with oil or dry, shall be shared equally among all the priests, Aharon's descendants.

**7-11** ~ "This is the law concerning a peace offering that is sacrificed to God. **7-12** ~ If it is offered as a thanksgiving offering, then it must be presented along with unleavened loaves mixed with oil, as well as flat matzot saturated with oil, and also loaves of boiled flour mixed with oil. **7-13** ~ The sacrifice shall also be presented along with loaves of leavened bread. All of these shall be presented together with one's thanksgiving-peace offering.

**7-14** ~ "From each one of these four bread offerings he shall present one-tenth of that offering as an elevated gift to God. This shall belong to the priest who sprinkles the blood of the peace offering.

# VAYIKRA / LEVITICUS – TZAV

*(in His nature as Source of Mercy)*

**7-15** ~ "The flesh of the thanksgiving-peace offering must be eaten completely on the day it is offered. None of it may be left over until the morning. **7-16** ~ However, if a person has brought a sacrifice meant merely to fulfill a general vow (*a neder*) or a specific pledge (*a nedevah*), he shall eat it on the same day that he offers his sacrifice and he may even leave over a portion to be eaten the next day. **7-17** ~ Even so, he may not leave over any portion for the third day but must burn it in fire. **7-18** ~ Should the person bringing the offering merely be thinking of eating it on the third day this sacrifice will not be accepted. It is considered disgusting and will be rejected by God. Any person who eats the sacrifice on the third day will bear his guilt by being separated from nearness to God.

**7-19** ~ "Any sacrificial flesh that comes in contact with something ritually unclean may not be eaten; it must be burned in fire. Otherwise, this flesh is acceptable and may be eaten by any ritually clean person. **7-20** ~ Should a ritually unclean person eat the flesh of a peace sacrifice to God his soul will be cut off from his people.

**7-21** ~ "Any person who comes in contact with human ritual uncleanness, or with an unclean animal or other unclean creature, and then eats the flesh of a peace offering to God, his soul will be cut off from his people."

**7-22** ~ God spoke to Moshe, telling him **7-23** ~ to relate the following to the Yisra'elites:

# VAYIKRA / LEVITICUS – TZAV

*(in His nature as Source of Mercy)*

"Do not eat any of the hard fat cut from the sacrifice of an ox, sheep, or goat.  7-24 ~ But if an animal is improperly slaughtered or fatally wounded you may use its hard fat for any purpose you desire, except that you may not eat it.  7-25 ~ Anyone who eats of this hard fat from any animal offered to God, his soul will be cut off from his people.

7-26 ~ "Do not consume any blood, whether from a mammal or a bird, no matter where you may live.  7-27 ~ Any person who eats blood shall have his soul cut off from his people."

7-28 ~ God spoke to Moshe, telling him  7-29 ~ to relate the following to the Yisra'elites:

"When anyone brings a peace offering to God he must remove from it a special portion to present to God.  7-30 ~ He must himself bring these parts to the priest. The priest shall present these as a fire offering in the following manner. The priest shall first place his hands beneath the hands of the owner and together they shall move the offering in the prescribed motions as a wave offering before God. The priest shall then place these parts upon the animal's chest.

7-31 ~ "Next, the priest shall burn these choice parts on the altar. The animal's chest, however, shall not be burned but shall belong to Aharon and his descendants.

# VAYIKRA / LEVITICUS – TZAV

*(in His nature as Source of Mercy)*

7-32 ~ "The right hind leg of the peace offerings also shall be given as a gift to the priests, in recognition of their position. 7-33 ~ This right hind leg shall be given to any descendant of Aharon fit to offer the blood and fat of the peace offerings. 7-34 ~ This is because I have separated from the peace sacrifices of Yisra'elites the chest as a wave offering and the hind leg as an elevated gift from them and I have given these parts to Aharon and his descendants. It is a law for all time that this portion be taken from the Yisra'elites.

7-35 ~ "This is the same as that portion of God-s fire offerings that were given on the day Aharon and his sons were anointed as priests to God. 7-36 ~ On that day that God anointed them He commanded that this portion be given to them by the Yisra'elites. It is a law for all time that this portion be taken from the Yisra'elites and given to Aharon and his descendants.

7-37 ~ "This, then, is the law of the burnt offering, the meal offering, the sin offering, the inauguration offering, and the peace offering, 7-38 ~ which God gave to Moshe on Mount Sinai. It was given on the day that He commanded the Yisra'elites to offer their sacrifices to God in the Sinai Desert."

8-1 ~ God spoke these words to Moshe:

# VAYIKRA / LEVITICUS – TZAV

*(in His nature as Source of Mercy)*

**8-2** ~ "Take Aharon and his sons, and jointly with them gather together the vestments, the anointing oil, the sin offering bull, the two rams, and the basket of unleavened bread. **8-3** ~ Summon the entire community to come to the entrance of the Communion Tent."

**8-4** ~ Moshe did as God had commanded, and the community assembled at the entrance to the Communion Tent.

**8-5** ~ Moshe said to the community, "This is what God has commanded to be done." **8-6** ~ Moshe now brought forth Aharon and his sons and immersed them in a ritual pool, a mikvah. **8-7** ~ He then dressed Aharon in the tunic, belted him with the sash, put the robe on him, and placed the ephod over it. He next bound the ephod in place with its belt. **8-8** ~ Then he placed the breastplate on Aharon over the ephod, The Urim and Thumin, complete with their stones set in place, were now positioned in the breastplate. **8-9** ~ He set the turban on Aharon's head. He then set the gold forehead plate as a sacred coronet on Aharon's forehead just below the turban, The robing of Aharon was now complete, as God had commanded Moshe.

**8-10** ~ Moshe took the anointing oil and with it he sanctified the Tabernacle and everything in it. **8-11** ~ Seven times he sprinkled oil on the altar. After anointing the alter he then made holy the altar's utensils and the washstand with its base.

# VAYIKRA / LEVITICUS – TZAV

*(in His nature as Source of Mercy)*

**8**-12 ~ Moshe poured some of the anointing oil on Aharon's head and sanctified him. **8**-13 ~ He then brought forth Aharon's sons and dressed them in their priestly tunics, girded them with sashes, and placed their hats upon their heads. It was all done as God had commanded Moshe.

**8**-14 ~ Moshe brought forth the bull for the sin offering, and Aharon and his sons pressed their hands heavily on the head of the animal. **8**-15 ~ Moshe then slaughtered it and collected the blood in a vessel. He dipped his finger in the blood, then touched each of the altar's horn-shaped projections, thus purifying the altar. He poured the rest of the blood onto its base. In this way the altar was sanctified so that atonement could be offered on it.

**8**-16 ~ From the sin offering Moshe took the fat that was on the stomachs, the lobe of the liver, and the kidneys along with their fat, and he burned them on the altar. **8**-17 ~ All the rest of the bull, its skin, flesh and insides, he burned in fire outside the camp. It was all done as God had commanded Moshe.

**8**-18 ~ Moshe brought forward the ram for the burnt offering, and Aharon and his sons pressed their hands heavily on the head of the animal. **8**-19 ~ Moshe slaughtered it and then dashed the blood on all sides of the altar. **8**-20 ~ Next, he cut the ram into pieces, then on the altar he burned the head, these cut pieces, and the fatty intestinal membrane **8**-21 ~ which

*(in His nature as Source of Mercy)*

had been removed after the intestines and legs had been scrubbed with water. Moshe thus burned the entire ram on the altar as a burnt offering. This fire offering was a pleasing fragrance to God, and it was all done as God had commanded Moshe.

**8**-22 ~ Moshe brought forth the second ram as an installation ram. Aharon and his sons pressed their hands heavily on the head of the animal. **8**-23 ~ Moshe slaughtered the ram and took some of its blood and placed it on Aharon's right ear on a particular spot told to him, also on Aharon's right thumb, and on Aharon's right big toe.

**8** 24 ~ Moshe brought forward Aharon's sons. He took some of the ram's blood and placed it on their right ears on a particular spot told to him, on their right thumbs, and on their right big toes. From the remaining blood Moshe then sprinkled some on all sides of the altar.

**8**-25 ~ Moshe next gathered the choice portions, these being: the broad tail, all the fat that covers the stomachs, the lobe of the liver, the two kidneys along with their fat, and the right hind leg, **8**-26 ~ From the basket of unleavened bread he took one loaf of unleavened bread, one loaf of oil bread, and one flat loaf. In the presence of God He placed these loaves on the choice portions and on the right leg.

**8**-27 ~ Moshe lifted all of these and placed them in Aharon's hands and in the hands of Aharon's sons. He waved them in the manner he was taught

# VAYIKRA / LEVITICUS – TZAV

*(in His nature as Source of Mercy)*

as a wave offering before God.  **8**-28 ~ Moshe then took the wave offering from their hands and burned it on the altar together with the burnt offering. This was the installation offering, a pleasing fragrance, a fire offering to God.

**8**-29 ~ Moshe took the ram's chest and made his own wave offering before God with this portion of the installation ram, all the motions done as God had commanded him.

**8**-30 ~ Moshe now took some of the anointing oil together with the remaining blood from the sprinkling on the altar, and he sprinkled it on Aharon and Aharon's vestments, as well as on Aharon's sons and their vestments.  In this manner he sanctified Aharon and his sons and all their vestments.

**8**-31 ~ Moshe said to Aharon and his sons, "Cook the flesh at the entrance to the Communion Tent.  There you shall eat it, along with the bread in the installation basket.  This you shall do because I have given this instruction to you and to your sons.  **8**-32 ~ Whatever is left over of the flesh and the bread you shall burn in fire.

**8**-33 ~ "Do not leave the entrance of the Communion Tent for seven days, but remain there until the seven-day period of the inauguration ceremony is complete.  **8**-34 ~ It has been commanded by God that whatever has been done on the first day shall be done on all seven days of the inauguration period to atone for you.  **8**-35 ~ For seven days and seven nights you shall remain at the entrance of the Communion Tent. Keep this commandment given to you by God and you shall not die."

**8**-36 ~ Aharon and his sons did all as God had commanded them through Moshe.

## VAYIKRA / LEVITICUS – SHEMINI
### Understanding this Holy Book

**Targum Americana,** as much as is possible in English, maintains the majesty of the Holy language of the Torah. It is not a translation but an interpretation, verse by verse, based on over 2,000 years of understandings offered by its original interpreters and the great later Jewish Sages and commentators.

Study of this work is not a substitute for learning Torah in the original Holy Language. Learning Torah without the clarifications of the Sages and commentators surely will lead to gross errors in understanding.

# VAYIKRA / LEVITICUS – SHEMINI

*(in His nature as Source of Mercy)*

**9-1** ~ On the day following the seven days of installment, Moshe summoned Aharon, his sons, and the elders of Yisra'el. **9-2** ~ He said to Aharon, "Take an unblemished yearling calf for yourself to make a sin offering, and an unblemished ram to make a burnt offering, as sacrifices before God. **9-3** ~ Speak to the Yisra'elites and tell them to take an unblemished goat for a sin offering, an unblemished yearling calf and an unblemished goat for a burnt offering, **9-4** ~ and an unblemished bull and an unblemished ram for peace offerings. These they shall sacrifice before God along with a meal offering mixed with oil, for God will reveal Himself to them today."

**9-5** ~ They brought to the front of the Communion Tent everything that Moshe had ordered them to bring, and the entire community came forth and stood before God.

**9-6** ~ Moshe said, "This is what God has commanded: Do as He has commanded and God's glory will be revealed to you."

**9-7** ~ Moshe then said to Aharon, "Come up to the altar and prepare your sin offering and burnt offering, thus atoning for you and the people. To complete the people's atonement, also prepare the people's offering as God has commanded."

**9-8** ~ Aharon went up to the altar and there slaughtered the calf he had brought for the sin offering. **9-9** ~ Aharon's sons collected the blood and

*(in His nature as Source of Mercy)*

brought it to Aharon, who dipped his finger in the blood and placed some on each of the altar's horn-shaped projections.  He spilled the rest of the blood on the altar's base.  **9-10** ~ Aharon then burned the fat, the kidneys and the lobe of the liver of the sin offering.   It was all done as God had commanded Moshe.  **9-11** ~ Aharon then burned the flesh and the skin of the sin offering in a place outside the camp.

**9-12** ~  He slaughtered the burnt offering.  Then Aharon's sons collected the blood and brought it to Aharon, who dashed the blood on all sides of the altar.  **9-13** ~  They passed the cut up parts of the burnt offering to Aharon, piece by piece, along with the head.  These Aharon burned on the altar.  **9-14** ~  He washed the entrails and the feet and burned them on the altar with the rest of the burnt offering.

**9-15** ~  Aharon now brought forth the people's offering.  He took the goat for the sin offering and slaughtered it.  He then prepared it in the same manner as the first sin offering.  **9-16** ~  He brought forth all the parts for the burnt offering and prepared them according to the law.

**9-17** ~  He brought forth the grain offering and gathered some with his three middle fingers of one hand.  This he then burned on the altar in addition to the morning's regular grain offering.

**9-18** ~  Aharon slaughtered the bull and the ram of the people's peace sacrifices.  Aharon's sons passed the blood to him and he dashed it on all

*(in His nature as Source of Mercy)*

sides of the altar. **9**-19 ~ They also passed to him the choice parts of the bull and the ram, these being the broad tail, the fatty membrane, the kidneys and the lobe of the liver. **9**-20 ~ They placed these choice parts on the chests of the slaughtered animals. Aharon burned the choice parts on the altar **9**-21 ~ after first waving the chests and right hind legs in the prescribed manner as a wave offering before God. Aharon and his sons did all as God had commanded them through Moshe.

**9**-22 ~ Aharon lifted his hands toward the people and blessed them with the Priestly Blessing. He then descended from the altar where he had prepared the sin offering, the burnt offering, and the peace offerings.

**9**-23 ~ Moshe and Aharon went into the Communion Tent, and when they came out they blessed the people. Then, in the light of a fire, God's glory was revealed to all the people. **9**-24 ~ Fire came above the Holy of Holies and consumed the burnt offering and the choice parts on the altar. When the people saw this they became ecstatic and raised their voices in praise and lowered their heads and bowed down to the ground.

**10**-1 ~ Aharon's sons, Nadav and Avihu, each took his fire pan and placed hot coals and incense on it but this was not as commanded and explained to them. They each offered it before God although it was not authorized. **10**-2 ~ Fire came down from the sky by God's hand and they were consumed and died before God.

## VAYIKRA / LEVITICUS – SHEMINI

*(in His nature as Source of Mercy)*

**10**-3 ~ Moshe said to Aharon, "This is what God meant when He said, "I will be sanctified, pure and holy, among those close to Me, and in this way I shall be glorified in their eyes." Aharon remained silent.

**10**-4 ~ Moshe summoned Mishael and Eltzafan, the sons of Aharon's uncle Uzziel, and said to them, "Enter the Sanctuary and remove the bodies of Nadav and Avihu from there. Bring them outside the camp." **10**-5 ~ They did as they were directed by Moshe, placing the bodies in their tunics and carrying them outside the camp.

**10**-6 ~ Moshe said to Aharon and to his remaining sons, Eleazar and Ithamar, "Do not go without your hair being well trimmed because you are now high priests. Do not tear your vestments or unravel its stitches, for this will bring divine wrath upon the entire community. and you will die by the hand of God. As for your brothers, let the entire community, the family of Yisra'el, mourn for these two who were burned by God. **10**-7 ~ Do not leave the entrance of the Communion Tent while God's anointing oil is still upon you, for then you will die by the hand of God,"

All that Moshe said they did.

**10**-8 ~ God spoke to Aharon these words; **10**-9 ~ "Neither you nor any of your descendants may drink wine or any other liquid that could make you drunk, for then you shall die by the hand of God. This is a law for all time. **10**-10 ~ When you do not drink a strong drink you will be able to distinguish between the holy and the common, and between the ritually

*(in His nature as Source of Mercy)*

unclean and the clean.  **10**-11 ~ You will be able to render true decisions as a judge for the Yisra'elites in all the laws that God has taught you through Moshe."

**10**-12 ~ Moshe now spoke to Aharon and his surviving sons, Eleazar and Ithamar, concerning their offerings: "Bring the remainder of the meal offering you brought before God near the altar and eat it there as unleavened bread.  Since it is a holy of holies  **10**-13 ~ you must eat it only in a holy place.  I have been commanded to explain to you that this is the portion allotted to you and your descendants from God's fire offerings.

**10**-14 ~ "However, the chest taken as a wave offering and the hind leg taken as an elevated offering you are permitted eat together with your sons and daughters.  It is the portion designated for you and your descendants from the peace sacrifices of the Yisra'elites.

**10**-15 ~ "The hind leg for the elevated gift and the chest for the wave offering shall be set on top of the choice parts designated as the fire offering.  All of these shall be waved in the prescribed manner of the  wave offering.   The leg and the chest are intended for you and your descendants for all time, as God has commanded."

**10**-16 ~ Moshe then inquired of the priests about the goat slaughtered as a sin offering.  When he discovered that it had already been burned he became angry with Aharon's sons, Eleazar and Ithamar.  He said to them, **10**-17 ~ "Why did you eat the sin offering in a place that was not holy?

# VAYIKRA / LEVITICUS – SHEMINI

*(in His nature as Source of Mercy)*

This offering is a holy of holies that was given to you to remove the community's guilt and to atone for them before God.  **10-18** ~ Since its blood was not brought into the Inner Sanctuary, you should have eaten it in a holy place as I commanded you."

**10-19** ~ Aharon responded to Moshe, "Today, when my sons Nadav and Avihu sacrificed their sin offering and burnt offering before God, and they were consumed by God's fire, would it have been right in God's eyes to eat the sin offering?"

**10-20** ~ When Moshe heard this, he approved of what Aharon had done.

**11**-1 ~ God spoke to Moshe and Aharon, telling them  **11**-2 ~ to speak to the Yisra'elites and be sure that they understood the following:

"Of all the animals in the world these are the ones that you may eat:

**11-3** ~ "Among mammals, you may eat any of them that has completely split hooves and brings up its cud.  **11-4** ~ However, there are cud-chewing, hoofed animals that you may not eat. These are:

"The camel. It is ritually unclean to you although it brings up its cud, because it does not have a true split hoof.

**11-5** ~ "The hyrax. It is ritually unclean to you although it brings up its cud, because it does not have a true split hoof.

# VAYIKRA / LEVITICUS – SHEMINI

*(in His nature as Source of Mercy)*

**11-6** ~ "The hare/rabbit.  It is ritually unclean to you although it brings up its cud, because it does not have a true split hoof.

**11-7** ~ "The pig.  It is ritually unclean to you although it has a true split hoof, because it does not bring up its cud,

**11-8** ~ "Do not eat any part of these animals.  Neither may you touch the carcass any of these animals for they are ritually unclean to you, and their touch shall defile you and make you ritually unclean.

**11-9** ~ "Of all the creatures in the water these are the ones that you may eat:

"You may eat any creature that that lives in the water, whether in salt water or fresh water, as long as it has fins and scales.

**11-10** ~ "On the other hand, all such creatures that do not have fins and scales, whether or not they are considered fish, are loathsome to you and must be shunned.  **11-11** ~ They must forever be avoided by not eating their flesh.  **11-12** ~ I repeat, every aquatic creature without fins and scales must be shunned.

**11-13** ~ "There are flying creatures that you must avoid.  Do not eat the flesh of these:

# VAYIKRA / LEVITICUS – SHEMINI

*(in His nature as Source of Mercy)*

Carrion-eating birds such as the eagle and the griffin vulture;  **11-14** ~ the ossifrage bone breaker bird; such fish catching birds as the osprey and the fish hawk; meat eaters such as the kite; the vulture and buzzard and their like;  **11-15** ~ the raven and crow and their like; **11-16** ~ all the like of the ostrich, owl, gull and hawk;  **11-17** ~ the falcon; the cormorant; the ibis; **11-18** ~ the swan; birds which vomit up their prey such as the pelican; the magpie;  **11-19** ~ the stork; such large red-crested birds as the hoopoe and the large grouse; and the bat.

**11-20** ~ "Every flying insect, with but one exception, that uses four legs for walking, even if it has more than four legs, shall be avoided by you.  **11-21** ~ The one exception is any insect that has knees extending prominently above its feet, using these legs to hop on the ground.  **11-22** ~ Among these insects are the red or desert locust and their like, the yellow or bald locust and their like, the spotted grey locust or large long-horned grasshopper and their like, and the small white locust and their like *(but only the Yemenites have retained the skill to recognize these swarming insects)*.  **11-23** ~ All other flying insects that use four legs for walking you must avoid.

11-24 ~ "You have been told of those animals whose carcasses will defile you when they are touched,  This will make you ritually unclean until you have immersed your body that evening in a ritual pool, a mikvah. **11-25** ~ Moreover, should you lift the carcass you will have to immerse even your clothing and, as well, remain ritually unclean until evening.

# VAYIKRA / LEVITICUS – SHEMINI

*(in His nature as Source of Mercy)*

11-26 ~ "You now understand that every animal that has true hooves but does not bring up its cud is ritually unclean to you and anyone touching its flesh shall become ritually unclean.

11-27 ~ "Similarly, any animal that walks on its paws or hands among the four-footed animals shall be ritually unclean to you, and anyone touching its carcass shall become ritually unclean until evening. 11-28 ~ Furthermore, should a person lift the carcass he will have to immerse even his clothing and, as well, remain ritually unclean until evening. In this way are they ritually unclean to you.

11-29 ~ "Ritually unclean to you are the smaller animals and creeping creatures that breed on land: the weasel, mole, rat, ferret, and field mouse; the snake, lizard, toad, and salamander; 11-30 ~ the hedgehog, beaver, gecko, and skink; and the snail. 11-31 ~ These are the small animals that are ritually unclean to you, and anyone touching their carcass shall become ritually unclean until he immerses that evening in a ritual pool, a mikvah.

11-32 ~ "If any of these dead animals falls on anything with which work is done, such as wooden vessels, clothing, leather goods, or sacks, that article shall become ritually unclean and remain ritually unclean until it is immersed that evening in a ritual pool, a mikvah.

11-33 ~ "If any of these dead animals falls into a clay vessel, or even enters the inside space of a clay vessel, the vessel becomes contaminated.

# VAYIKRA / LEVITICUS – SHEMINI

*(in His nature as Source of Mercy)*

Anything contained within the inside space of this vessel also is contaminated. The clay vessel can not be purified; it must be broken. 11-34 ~ Any food normally consumed by humans that has ever become wet with water, dew, olive oil, wine, milk, blood or date honey also can become ritually unclean should this food enter the inside space of a contaminated clay vessel.

11-35 ~ "Any of these carcasses touching finished clay vessels, or even a clay oven or range once it has been used, becomes ritually unclean. It must be broken because it can never be made unclean.

11-36 ~ "Only the waters of a mikvah can remain forever ritually clean, whether it is of a man made pit or a natural spring. Any other waters that are touched by the dead body of one of these creatures shall become ritually unclean.

11-37 ~ "Any of these carcasses touching an edible seed which has been planted does not contaminate the seed. 11-38 ~ However, should the unplanted seed become wet with water, dew, olive oil, wine, milk, blood or date honey, from that time onward any of these carcasses touching this seed does contaminate the seed and it becomes ritually unclean to you.

11-39 ~ "If any permitted animal dies before its ritual slaughter, anyone touching its carcass shall become ritually unclean until evening. 11-40 ~ Anyone eating any part of such a carcass shall become ritually unclean.

## VAYIKRA / LEVITICUS – SHEMINI

*(in His nature as Source of Mercy)*

He must immerse himself as well as his clothing in a ritual pool, a mikvah, and he will remain unclean until evening.

**11-41** ~ "Every small animal that breeds on land shall be avoided and shall not be eaten. **11-42** ~ This means that you may not eat any small creature that crawls on its belly, or that has four or more feet and also breeds on land. All such creatures must be avoided. **11-43** ~ Do not contaminate yourselves by eating any small creature that breeds on the land. Do not defile yourselves with them, for it will bring disgust upon you. **11-44** ~ As I am God, your Lord, and as I am holy, since you are made in My image you must also make yourselves holy and remain sanctified. Therefore I repeat, do not contaminate yourselves by eating any small creature that breeds on the land.

**11-45** ~ "I am God, and I brought you out of Egypt to be your God. Therefore, since I am holy so, too, must you remain holy.

**11-46** ~ "This then is the law concerning mammals, birds, creatures of the sea, and the small creeping creatures. **11-47** ~ With My giving you this law you will be able to distinguish between the acceptable and the unclean, between animals you may eat and animals you may not eat."

## VAYIKRA / LEVITICUS – TAZRIA
## Understanding this Holy Book

**Targum Americana,** as much as is possible in English, maintains the majesty of the Holy language of the Torah.  It is not a translation but an interpretation, verse by verse, based on over 2,000 years of understandings offered by its original interpreters and the great later Jewish Sages and commentators.

Study of this work is not a substitute for learning Torah in the original Holy Language. Learning Torah without the clarifications of the Sages and commentators surely will lead to gross errors in understanding.

# VAYIKRA / LEVITICUS – TAZRIA

*(in His nature as Source of Mercy)*

**12**-1 ~ God spoke to Moshe, telling him   **12**-2 ~ to say the following to the Yisra'elites:

"When a woman conceives and gives birth to a boy, she shall be ritually unclean for seven days, just as she is ritually unclean during the time that she is separated from her husband when she has her periodic discharge.  **12**-3 ~ On the eighth day the child's foreskin shall be circumcised.  **12**-4 ~ Then, for an additional thirty-three days, making a total of forty days of her purification period, she shall remain ritually unclean.  Until this period is complete she shall not touch anything holy, and she shall not enter the Sanctuary.

**12**-5 ~ "If she gives birth to a girl he shall be ritually unclean for two weeks, just as she is ritually unclean during the time she is separated from her husband when she has her periodic discharge.  Then, for an additional sixty-six days, making a total of eighty days of her purification period, she shall remain ritually unclean.

**12**-6 ~ "When her purification period is complete, whether for a son or a daughter, she shall bring to the priest at the entrance of the Communion Tent a yearling sheep for a burnt offering.  Also, for a sin offering she shall bring a young common dove whose feathers have not yet begun to glisten, or a turtle dove.  **12**-7 ~ The priest shall offer thes sacrifices before God and atone for the woman, thereby cleansing her of the blood of her womb.  This law applies whether the woman gives birth to a boy or a girl.

# VAYIKRA / LEVITICUS – TAZRIA

*(in His nature as Source of Mercy)*

**12**-8 ~ "If the woman can not afford a sheep, she shall bring two turtle doves, one for a burnt offering and one for a sin offering. The priest shall make atonement for her and she shall be ritually clean."

**13**-1 ~ God spoke to Moshe and Aharon, saying:

**13**-2 ~ "If a person has a white blotch the color of clean, white wool and it has the appearance of being raised; or a discoloration of a duller color than this, more like the color of egg membrane; or a shiny pink or white spot that has the appearance of being below the skin surface, and it is at least the size of a large bean; and any of these is suspected of being the tzaraas affliction which occurs because of gossip or slander, he shall be brought to Aharon or one of his descendants who is a priest. **13**-3 ~ The priest shall examine the mark on the person's skin. If two hairs on the mark have turned white, and if it is a discoloration or spot that appears to have penetrated the skin below the surface, then it is the tzaraas curse. As soon as the priest sees it he shall declare the person spiritually unclean.

**13**-4 ~ "However, if there is a white spot on the skin but it does not appear to have penetrated the skin below the surface, and its hairs have not turned white, then it is an uncertain affliction. The priest shall mark a circle around the spot and quarantine the person for seven days. **13**-5 ~ The priest shall examine the person on the seventh day and if the mark has not increased in size, the priest shall quarantine the person for an additional seven days. **13**-6 ~ The priest shall then examine the victim again. If the

# VAYIKRA / LEVITICUS – TAZRIA

*(in His nature as Source of Mercy)*

mark has faded but still can be seen, or if the color has changed to a duller white, or if the spot has not spread, the priest shall declare that the spot is not a tzaraas affliction; the spot is an ordinary white condition of some kind. The person still must immerse his body and clothing in a ritual pool and he is then ritually clean.

**13-7** ~ "However, if after the priest has purified the person, the person examines the white patch on the skin and sees that it has increased in size he must show it to the priest again. **13-8** ~ If the priest also sees that the patch has increased in size, he shall declare the person spiritually unclean, for it is the tzaraas curse.

**13-9** · "When a person is suspected of having the tzaraas curse he shall be brought to the priest. **13-10** ~ If the priest sees that there is a white blotch on the skin that is the color of a tzaraas affliction, and it has turned the hair within it white, or if there is such a white blotch that has an area at least the size of a lentil within the blotch that clearly looks different, **13-11** ~ it is an old tzaraas curse. The priest must then declare the person spiritually unclean. He need not quarantine the person since he is clearly spiritually unclean.

**13-12** ~ "This is the law if the small afflicted area spreads over the skin to cover the person completely, from head to foot, wherever the priest shall be able to view it. But the priest shall not examine the hidden places and crevices of the body. **13-13** ~ When the priest sees that the discoloration has covered all of the person's skin, he shall declare the afflicted

# VAYIKRA / LEVITICUS – TAZRIA

person spiritually clean. As long as he has turned completely white he is spiritually clean. **13**-14 ~ However, should healthy skin appear on the person he has become spiritually unclean **13**-15 ~ and the priest shall declared it so. That he now has an area of healthy skin is a sign of the uncleanness of the tzaraas curse. **13**-16 ~ If the healthy skin turns white again the person shall return to the priest. **13**-17 ~ When the priest sees that the afflicted area has turned completely white, the priest shall declare him clean and he is then ritually pure.

**13**-18 ~ "This is the law when there is an infection, such as a pustule, boil or blister which has not been caused by a burn, and it has then healed. **13**-19 ~ If a white blotch or a light but clearly pink spot then develops on the area where the infection was, it must be shown to the priest. **13**-20 ~ The priest shall examine it, and if has the appearance of being below the skin surface and its hair has turned white, it is the tzaraas curse that has erupted over the infection.

**13**-21 ~ "However, if the priest examines it and it does not have white hair, and it does not have the appearance of being below the skin surface, and it is a dull white color, the priest shall quarantine the person for seven days. **13**-22 ~ If this spot then increases in size, the priest shall declare the person spiritually unclean, for it is the tzaraas curse.

**13**-23 ~ "If after quarantine the spot remains stable and does not expand, it is scar tissue from the infection, or an ordinary inflammation, and the priest shall declare him clean and he is then ritually pure.

# VAYIKRA / LEVITICUS – TAZRIA

*(in His nature as Source of Mercy)*

**13**-24 ~ "This is the law when a bright pink or white spot appears where there was a burn that has healed. **13**-25 ~ The priest shall examine it, and if has the appearance of being below the skin surface and its hair has turned white, it is the tzaraas curse that has erupted over the healed burn. Because it is the tzaraas curse the priest must declare the person spiritually unclean.

**13**-26 ~ "However, if the priest examines it and it does not have white hair, and it does not have the appearance of being below the skin surface, and it is a dull white color, the priest shall quarantine the person for seven days. **13**-27 ~ On the seventh day if this spot has increased in size, the priest shall declare the person spiritually unclean, for it is the tzaraas curse.

**13**-28 ~ "However, if after quarantine the spot remains stable and does not expand, or if it has faded, even if the spot has expanded, it is a discoloration from the burn and the priest shall declare him clean and he is then ritually pure.

**13**-29 ~ "This is the law concerning a man or woman with an affliction on the head or hair of the face. **13**-30 ~ The priest shall examine it to see if the skin has a discoloration and the appearance of being below the skin surface. If this is so and it is clear that hair within the spot has either fallen out or broken off, or it has only short, fine blond hairs in it, the priest must declare the person spiritually unclean. Such a bald-appearing mark is the tzaraas curse.

# VAYIKRA / LEVITICUS – TAZRIA

*(in His nature as Source of Mercy)*

**13-31** ~ "However, if the priest sees that the bald-appearing patch does not have the appearance of being below the skin surface, but it does not have dark hair in it, the priest shall quarantine the person so afflicted for seven days. **13-32** ~ If after these seven days the spot has remained stable and has not expanded, and there is no blond hair in it, **13-33** ~ the afflicted person shall shave himself but he shall leave the patch untouched. The priest shall quarantine the person so afflicted for an additional seven days.

**13-34** ~ "After these additional days of quarantine the priest shall examine the affliction. If it has not increased in size, or if it does not have the appearance of being below the skin surface, the priest shall declare him spiritually clean and he is then ritually pure. The person still must immerse his body and clothing in a ritual pool and he is then ritually clean.

**13-35** ~ "However, if after he has immersed and been declared ritually clean he sees that the patch has increased in size, **13-36** ~ the priest must examine the patch to affirm that it has indeed expanded. If he confirms this, he need not look for short, fine blond hairs in it for it is unquestionably the tzaraas curse. **13-37** ~ But if the bald-appearing patch has remained unchanged or has faded and appears to be normal skin, and the patch has grown dark hairs within it, it is healed skin and the priest shall declare him clean and he is then ritually pure.

**13-38** ~ "If the skin on the body of a man or woman becomes covered with white spots, **13-39** ~ the priest shall examine the spots. If these are merely dull, discolored spots then it is a simple rash breaking out on the

*(in His nature as Source of Mercy)*

skin and it is clean.

**13-40** ~ "If a man loses the hair toward the back of his head it is simple baldness. He is clean. **13-41** ~ If likewise he loses hair on his head nearer his face it is merely a receding hairline. He is clean.

**13-42** ~ "But if he has a bright pink spot on his balding area or where his hairline has receded, it may be a sign of the tzaraas curse. **13-43** ~ The priest shall examine it to confirm that the spot is the bright pink of the tzaraas curse. **13-44** ~ If it is confirmed as so then the person is afflicted with the tzaraas curse and he is spiritually unclean. Because of these signs the priest must declare him spiritually unclean.

**13-45** ~ "When the person is thus afflicted and has been declared unclean, his clothing must have a tear made in it as if he is in mourning, he must go without a haircut, and he must cover his head down to his lips. Moreover, he must call out "Unclean! Unclean!" wherever he goes. **13-46** ~ As long as he has the tzaraas mark he shall remain unclean. Because he is unclean he must remain alone, and he must reside outside the camp.

**13-47** ~ "This is the law when there is a tzaraas mark on a garment. This is for any white garment of wool, linen, or a combination of wool and linen. **13-48** ~ Also, should only the warp thread or only the woof thread of the garment be white, then even if the mark is only on the warp threads or only on the woof threads, or if there is a mark on a garment of leather or

*(in His nature as Source of Mercy)*

any other article made of leather, any of these articles may be contaminated. **13**-49 ~ If the mark appears as a bright green or bright yellow or bright red area on any of these articles or threads it may be a tzaraas mark, and it must be shown to the priest.

**13**-50 ~ "The priest shall examine the mark to fix it in his mind, and then quarantine the affected article for seven days. **13**-51 ~ On the seventh day the priest again shall examine the affected area. If the mark has spread on the affected article, then it is the tzaraas curse and the article is spiritually unclean. **13**-52 ~ No matter whether the mark is on the woven cloth or only on the warp or woof threads, or whether the article is made of wool or linen or leather, the article containing the spot of tzaraas plague must be destroyed by fire.

**13**-53 ~ "If on the seventh day the priest shall see that the mark has not spread on the affected article, **13**-54 ~ the priest shall order the article having the mark to be washed and scrubbed and then quarantined for another seven days. **13**-55 ~ When this second period of quarantine has been completed the priest shall examine the article. The priest shall examine a cloth garment especially closely if it is new and fluffy or old and worn to confirm that the mark is on the cloth itself. If the mark has not changed in appearance, then even if the spot has not spread, still it is the tzaraas curse and the article is spiritually unclean and it must be burned.

**13**-56 ~ "If the priest has examined it after washing, scrubbing and

*(in His nature as Source of Mercy)*

quarantine, and the mark has faded or it has changed color from red to green or green to red, then he shall tear away the mark, whether from the cloth, leather or threads.   **13-57** ~ If the mark re-appears, looking the same and in the place where it was before, it is the tzaraas infection. The entire article must then be burned completely.

**13-58** ~ "If scrubbing the article containing the mark removes the mark, the article shall be immersed in a ritual pool and it is then ritually clean.

**13-59** ~ "This completes the discussion of the law concerning the mark of the tzaraas infection in wool or linen cloth, in a warp or woof thread, or in any leather item, through which it is rendered clean or unclean."

## VAYIKRA / LEVITICUS – <u>METZORAH</u>
## Understanding this Holy Book

**<u>Targum Americana,</u>** as much as is possible in English, maintains the majesty of the Holy language of the Torah. It is not a translation but an interpretation, verse by verse, based on over 2,000 years of understandings offered by its original interpreters and the great later Jewish Sages and commentators.


Study of this work is not a substitute for learning Torah in the original Holy Language. Learning Torah without the clarifications of the Sages and commentators surely will lead to gross errors in understanding.

# VAYIKRA / LEVITICUS – METZORAH

*(in His nature as Source of Mercy)*

**14**-1 ~ God spoke to Moshe these words:

**14**-2 ~ "This is the law concerning the person who has the tzaraas affliction and has been instructed by the priest to reside outside the camp. **14**-3 ~ The priest shall go to the afflicted person and shall examine him to verify that the tzaraas mark has healed. **14**-4 ~ The priest shall then order that the following be brought to the person undergoing purification: two live birds with white breasts from among those birds that are not prohibited to you, a rod of cedar wood one cubit long, combed out unspun crimson wool weighing one shekel *(four hundred grains of barley by weight)*, and a hyssop branch at least one handbreadth long.

**14**-5 ~ "The priest shall order one bird to be slaughtered over a new clay bowl filled with spring water into which the bird's blood shall be made to fall. The bird shall then be buried. **14**-6 ~ He shall then tie the cedar rod and the hyssop together with the crimson wool and take this together with the live bird. These he shall dip into the bowl which is holding the spring water mixed with the blood of the slaughtered bird. **14**-7 ~ He shall then sprinkle this mixture seven times from the bowl onto the person being purified, either on the person's hand or on his forehead, thereby rendering him ritually clean. The living bird shall then be sent away to the fields.

**14**-8 ~ "The person undergoing purification shall immerse his

*(in His nature as Source of Mercy)*

clothing in a mikvah, and the priest shall shave off all the person's hair. The person shall then immerse himself in a mikvah, thereby completing the first part of the purification process. He may now return to the camp but for seven days he may not yet have intimate relations with his wife.

**14-9** ~ "On the seventh day the priest shall shave off all the person's hair. From his head, his face, his eyebrows, from all his body parts must his hair be shaved off. The person shall then immerse his clothing and himself in a mikvah and he is then ritually clean. However, his purification process is not yet complete.

**14-10** ~ "On the eighth day, he shall take two unblemished male sheep, one unblemished yearling female sheep, three-tenths of an ephah *(about 6 quarts)* of the finest grade wheat flour mixed with one log of olive oil. **14-11** ~ The priest who is conducting the purification process shall gather together these items and the person being purified and position them before God at the entrance to the Communion Tent.

**14-12** ~ "The priest shall take one male sheep and the log of oil as a guilt offering, and he shall wave them before God in the manner prescribed for a wave offering. **14-13** ~ He shall then slaughter the sheep in a holy place north of the altar, in the same place where burnt offerings and sin offerings are slaughtered. **14-14** ~ The priest shall take some of the blood from the guilt offering and place it on the right

*(in His nature as Source of Mercy)*

ear lobe, the right thumb, and the right big toe of the person undergoing purification.

**14-15** ~ "The priest shall take some of the log of oil and pour it onto his left palm or the left palm of another priest. **14-16** ~ He shall then dip his right forefinger into this oil, and with this finger he shall sprinkle some oil seven times toward the Holy of Holies. **14-17** ~ The priest shall then place some of this oil onto the guilt offering's blood which previously had been placed on the right ear lobe, the right thumb, and the right big toe of the person undergoing purification. **14-18** ~ The priest shall then place the remaining oil onto the head of the person undergoing purification. In this way the priest shall make atonement for him before God.

**14-19** ~ "The priest shall then sacrifice the female sheep as a sin offering to remove the defilement from the person undergoing purification. After that he shall slaughter the second male sheep as a burnt offering. **14-20** ~ The priest shall then place the burnt offering and the meal offering on the alter for burning. The priest shall in this manner make atonement for him and he shall be ritually clean.

**14-21** ~ "If the afflicted person is poor and can not afford these sacrifices, he shall take one male sheep as a guilt offering, and it shall also serve as a wave offering to atone for him. He shall also take

# VAYIKRA / LEVITICUS – METZORAH

one-tenth of an ephah of the finest grade wheat flour mixed with one log of olive oil. **14-22** ~ In addition, he shall bring two turtle doves or two young common doves, whichever he can best afford, one for a sin offering and one for a burnt offering.

**14-23** ~ "On the eighth day of his purification, he shall offer these before God by bringing them to the priest at the entrance to the Communion Tent. **14-24** ~ The priest shall take the sheep of the guilt offering and the log of oil and he shall wave them in the prescribed manner as a wave offering before God. **14-25** ~ He shall slaughter the guilt offering sheep and collect its blood. This blood of the guilt offering he shall place on the right ear lobe, the right thumb, and the right big toe of the person undergoing purification.

**14-26** ~ "The priest shall then pour some of the oil onto his left palm or the left palm of another priest. **14-27** ~ With his right finger he shall sprinkle some of this oil seven times toward the Holy of Holies before God. **14-28** ~ The priest shall then place some of this oil onto the guilt offering's blood which previously had been placed on the right ear lobe, the right thumb, and the right big toe of the person undergoing purification. **14-28** ~ The priest shall then place the remaining oil onto the head of the person undergoing purification. In this way the priest shall make atonement for him before God.

# VAYIKRA / LEVITICUS – METZORAH

*(in His nature as Source of Mercy)*

**14-30** ~ "The priest shall then prepare either one of the two turtle doves or two young common doves that the person was able to afford. **14-31** ~ The priest shall take this offering and sacrifice it as a sin offering. The other bird he shall then take from the person and present it as a meal offering. The priest shall thus make atonement before God for the person undergoing purification.

**14-32** ~ "What you have just been told is the entire law concerning the person who has the mark of the tzaraas curse on him, and who can not afford the large animal sacrifices for his purification."

**14-33** ~ God spoke to Moshe these words:

**14-34** ~ "When you come to the land of your inheritance which I am giving to you, the land of Canaan, I will place a mark of the tzaraas curse on the houses in this land. **14-35** ~ The owner of the house shall come to the priest and tell him, 'There is a mark on my house that to me has the look of the tzaraas curse.'

**14-36** ~ "The priest shall give orders that the house be emptied out before any priest comes to see the mark. In this way everything that was in the house will not become spiritually unclean. Only then shall a priest come to view the mark..

**14-37** ~ "He shall examine the mark to determine if the mark on the wall of the house is a bright green or bright red streak, and the mark

*(in His nature as Source of Mercy)*

also appears either to have penetrated the surface, or it shows hairline cracking or appears to be an eroded area.

**14-38** ~ "If this is the appearance of the mark, the priest shall leave the house and stand just outside its entrance. The priest shall then quarantine the house for seven days. **14-39** ~ On the seventh day he shall return to examine it and determine if the mark has expanded on the wall of the house.

**14-40** ~ "He shall examine only ordinary building stones that are part of the walls of the house, but not any brick or marble or bedrock. If the mark has expanded on the ordinary building stones, the priest shall order the stones with the mark removed. Should these stones be part of a wall in common with a neighboring house, the priest shall order the neighbors to help with their removal. These marked stones, and any plaster which must be scraped from the stones and the area around the stones, shall be discarded to an unclean place outside the city. **14-41** ~ Other stones shall be brought to replace the removed stones. The owner shall then plaster with clay all the walls from which stones had been removed.

**14-43** ~ "After the stones have been replaced and the walls scraped and plastered, should the mark come back, **14-44** ~ the priest shall return and examine it. If the mark has returned and again has spread in the house, it is a tzaraas curse and the entire house is spiritually unclean. **14-45** ~ The priest shall now order the house to be

*(in His nature as Source of Mercy)*

demolished and all the material from the walls, whether stone, wood, or clay, shall be brought to an unclean place outside the city.

**14-46** ~ "As long as the house is in quarantine, anyone entering the house shall himself become unclean and must immerse himself in a mikvah. However, he shall remain unclean until the evening. **14-47** ~ If he remains in the quarantined house long enough to relax, especially as by sitting or lying down, he must immerse both himself and his clothing in a mikvah. If he remains in the house and eats even a small meal there, he must immerse both himself and his clothing in a mikvah.

**14-48** ~ "At the end of the seven days after the walls have been plastered, when the priest returns and sees that the mark has not returned in the house, the entire house shall then be declared clean by the priest.

**14-49** ~ "The final step in the purification process shall be for the priest to order two birds, a piece of cedar, some crimson wool, and a hyssop branch. **14-50** ~ He shall slaughter one bird over a clay bowl containing fresh spring water. **14-51** ~ He shall then take the piece of cedar, the hyssop, the crimson wool, and the live bird, and dip each in the blood of the slaughtered bird and in the fresh spring water, then sprinkle it seven times on the beam over the door of the house.

# VAYIKRA / LEVITICUS – METZORAH

*(in His nature as Source of Mercy)*

**14**-52 ~ "After the completion of this ceremony with the bird's blood and spring water and the live bird, and with the cedar wood, hyssop and crimson wool, the house becomes purified.  **14**-53 ~ The priest shall then send the live bird outside the city toward the fields. In this manner he shall make atonement for the house and it is then ritually clean.

**14**-54 ~ "You have now received the entire law for every tzaraas mark and bald patch on a person,  **14**-55 ~ every tzaraas mark in a garment or a house,  **14**-56 ~ and every white blotch, discoloration or spot on the skin,  **14**-57 ~ so that decisions can be properly made as to when the day is that a person, object or house is determined or restored to be ritually clean and when a person, object or house is determined to be ritually unclean.  This is the entire law concerning the tzaraas curse."

**15**-1 ~ God spoke to Moshe and Aharon, telling them  **15**-2 ~ to speak to the Yisra'elites and say this:

"When a man has a discharge from his sex organ, this discharge may render him spiritually unclean.  **15**-3 ~ He becomes unclean because of a discharge that dribbles a clear liquid, or a liquid with the appearance of the white of an unfertilized or spoiled egg or the appearance of the liquid seepage from barley dough.  This is so even if the discharge is too little to drip off his organ.

# VAYIKRA / LEVITICUS – METZORAH

(in His nature as Source of Mercy)

"This male discharge makes him spiritually unclean to the extent that **15-4** ~ anything he lies down upon or sits upon also becomes unclean. **15-5** ~ Any person who touches whatever a man with the discharge had lain upon must immerse himself and his clothing in a mikvah, yet he shall remain ritually unclean until evening. **15-6** ~ This is the same purification requirement even if he only sits upon whatever the person with the discharge had been sitting.

**15-7** ~ "If anyone touches the man with such a discharge, he, too, must immerse himself and his clothing in a mikvah, yet he shall remain ritually unclean until evening.

**15-8** ~ "If anyone comes in contact with the saliva of the person with such a discharge, he must immerse himself and his clothing in a mikvah, yet he shall remain ritually unclean until evening.

**15-9** ~ Any person with such a discharge renders the saddle he has ridden upon spiritually unclean. **15-10** ~ Thus, anyone touching something or lifting something that has been under a man who has had such a discharge shall become unclean himself. He must immerse himself and his clothing in a mikvah, yet he shall remain ritually unclean until evening.

**15-11** ~ "If anyone touches the man with such a discharge who has

# VAYIKRA / LEVITICUS – METZORAH

(in His nature as Source of Mercy)

not immersed even his hands in a mikvah, he, too, must immerse himself and his clothing in a mikvah, yet he shall remain ritually unclean until evening.

15-12 ~ "If the man with the discharge touches the inside of a clay vessel, or even just moves it, it must be broken. If it is a wooden vessel it must be cleaned of anything sticking to its surface and then immersed in a mikvah.

15-13 ~ "When the man is cleansed of his discharge, he must wait seven days for his purification. He shall then immerse his clothing and his body in a mikvah of running spring water. 15-14 ~ On the eighth day he shall take two turtle doves or two young common doves and bring them before God at the entrance of the Communion Tent. There he shall give the doves to the priest. 15-15 ~ The priest shall prepare one bird as a sin offering and one bird as a burnt offering. The priest shall thus make atonement before God for the man undergoing purification, thus purifying him of his discharge.

15-16 ~ "When a man discharges semen, he must immerse his entire body in a mikvah, yet he shall remain ritually unclean until evening. 15-17 ~ If any cloth or leather gets any semen on it, it must be immersed in a mikvah, yet it remains ritually unclean until evening.

# VAYIKRA / LEVITICUS – METZORAH

(in His nature as Source of Mercy)

**15-18** ~ "If a woman has intercourse with a man and he has a seminal discharge, both of them shall immerse in a mikvah, yet they shall remain ritually unclean until evening.

**15-19** ~ "When a woman has a bloody discharge of any kind from her womb, she becomes ritually unclean for seven days. Anyone touching her during this entire time similarly shall be ritually unclean, but only until that evening. **15-20** ~ As long as she is still in this menstrual state and has not completed purification, anything she lies down upon is unclean and anyone sitting upon this article also becomes unclean. **15-21** ~ Whoever touches her bed must immerse himself and his clothing in a mikvah, yet he shall remain ritually unclean until evening. **15-22** ~ Similarly, whoever sits upon any article upon which she has sat must immerse himself and his clothing in a mikvah, yet he shall remain ritually unclean until evening. **15-22** ~ Thus, if he has sat upon her bed or other article that she has sat upon, even if he has not directly touched it he is unclean until evening.

**15-24** ~ "If a man has intercourse with such a woman during her period of ritual impurity, this impurity is transferred to him and he shall be unclean for seven days. Any bed upon which he lies shall likewise be ritually unclean.

# VAYIKRA / LEVITICUS – METZORAH

(in His nature as Source of Mercy)

**15-25** ~ "If a woman has a discharge of blood anytime after her menstrual period has been completed, and it lasts for as many as three days, even if it happens immediately after she determines that her period has ended, then for as long as this discharge lasts she is considered as ritually unclean just as if it were during her natural menstrual cycle.  **15-26** ~ Thus, as long as she has the discharge, any bed upon which she lies shall become ritually unclean just as if she had been menstruating.  It also is the same for the articles she may sit on.  **15-27** ~ Anyone touching the bed or these articles must likewise immerse himself and his clothing in a mikvah, yet he shall remain ritually unclean until evening.

**15-28** ~ "When the woman's discharge has stopped, she must count seven days and only then can she undergo purification by immersion in a mikvah.  **15-29** ~ On the eighth day she shall bring to the entrance of the Communion Tent two turtle doves or two young common doves and there give to the priest.  **15-30** ~ The priest shall prepare one dove as a sin offering and the other dove as a burnt offering.  The priest thus shall make atonement for her before God. She shall then be purified from her spiritually unclean discharge.

**15-31** ~ "Moshe and Aharon, both of you must warn the Yisra'elites about their impurity, so that their impurity not cause

*(in His nature as Source of Mercy)*

them to die if they defile the Tabernacle that I have placed among them.

**15-32** ~ "This then is the entire law concerning the man who is spiritually unclean because of a discharge or a seminal emission, **15-33** ~ as well as the woman who has her monthly menstrual period, the man or woman who has a genital discharge, and the man who lies with a ritually unclean woman."

**16-1** ~ God spoke to Moshe right after the death of Aharon's two sons, who brought an unauthorized fire offering before God and they died. **16-2** ~ God said to Moshe:

"Speak to your brother, Aharon, and inform him that he may not enter the Sanctuary in a casual manner, nor so enter the Holy of Holies that is beyond the partition concealing the Ark. It is thus because I appear over the Ark cover in a cloud, and I do not want him to die because of this.

**16-3** ~ "When Aharon enters this Inner Sanctuary, it must be with a young bull for a sin offering and a ram for a burnt offering. **16-4** ~ When it is Yom Kippur, the Day of Atonement, he must put on four white linen vestments: a sanctified white linen tunic over linen pants; a linen sash he must don; and he must bind his head with a linen turban. Since these are sacred vestments, he must immerse himself in a mikvah before putting them on.

# VAYIKRA / LEVITICUS – METZORAH

*(in His nature as Source of Mercy)*

**16-5** ~ "From the Yisra'elite community he shall also take two goats for a sin offering, and one ram for a burnt offering.

**16-6** ~ "After the daily offering, he shall begin his own offerings by presenting his sin offering bull and atoning for himself and his family by confessing his sins. **16-7** ~ He shall then take the two goats and stand them before God at the entrance of the Communion Tent, one at his left side and one at his right side. **16-8** ~ Aharon shall place two pieces of boxwood into a box, to be used as lots. Upon one shall be written "for God" and upon the other shall be written "for Azazel". The box shall be shaken and then Aharon shall place both his hands in the box and take one lot in each hand. The lot in his left hand shall be placed on the goat at his left side, and the lot in his right hand shall be placed on the goat at his right side.

**16-9** ~ "The goat that has been selected by lot for God shall be presented by Aharon to be prepared for a sin offering. **16-9** ~ The goat selected by lot for Azazel shall remain alive. Aharon shall later make atonement upon it and send it to the Azazel rocky cliff area in the desert.

**16-11** ~ "Aharon shall present his sin offering bull, and make atonement for himself and his fellow priests. He shall then slaughter his bull as a sin offering.

# VAYIKRA / LEVITICUS – METZORAH

*(in His nature as Source of Mercy)*

**16**-12 ~ "He shall prepare a fire pan with a double handful of coals from the side of the sacrificial altar, along with a double handful of finely pulverized perfume incense, and bring them both into the Inner Sanctuary beyond the cloth partition. **16**-13 ~ There, before God, he shall place the incense on the fire to create smoke to spread over the cover of the Ark, which holds the stone tablets. He shall do this so as not to die.

**16**-14 ~ "He shall take some of the bull's blood and with his forefinger he shall sprinkle it once upward above the east side of the Ark cover. He shall then continue sprinkling the bull's blood with his forefinger downward seven times directly toward the Ark cover.

**16**-15 ~ "Now he shall slaughter the people's sin offering goat and bring its blood into the Inner Sanctuary beyond the cloth partition. With this blood he shall sprinkle it above and toward the Ark cover in the same manner as he had done with the bull's blood, **16**-16 ~ In this manner the priest shall make atonement for the Yisra'elites' defilement, that is, entering the Sanctuary or eating the sacrifice while ritually unclean, as well as for their rebellious acts and all their inadvertent misdeeds. The same ritual of sprinkling the blood of the bull and the blood of the goat shall be done in the Communion Tent for the entire Yisra'elite community, for they may have become ritually defiled in some other manner.

# VAYIKRA / LEVITICUS – METZORAH

*(in His nature as Source of Mercy)*

**16**-17 ~ "No one may be in the Communion Tent from the time that Aharon enters the Sanctuary to make atonement until the time he leaves. He shall be unaccompanied while he makes atonement for himself and for his family, and for the entire community of Yisra'el.

**16**-18 ~ "He shall then leave the Communion Tent and go out to the incense altar that is before God, and make atonement on it, He shall mix together some of the blood of the bull and of the goat and place the mixture on each of the horn-shaped projections of the incense altar, **16**-19 ~ He shall then sprinkle this mixture seven times with his forefinger onto the center of the altar. In this manner he shall purify and sanctify it from any defilement that may have been caused by the Yisra'elites.

**16**-20 ~ "When he has finished making atonement in the Inner Sanctuary, in the Communion Tent, and on the incense altar, he shall then present the live goat. **16**-21 ~ Aharon shall press both his hands on the live goat's head, and he shall confess all the Yisra'elites' sins, rebellious acts, and inadvertent misdeeds. Once he has placed these sins, rebellious acts, and inadvertent misdeeds on the goat's head, he shall send the goat into the desert accompanied by a man specially appointed for this task. **16**-22 ~ The goat will thus carry away all these sins to a desolate area in the desert.

# VAYIKRA / LEVITICUS – METZORAH

*(in His nature as Source of Mercy)*

**16**-23 ~ "Aharon shall then go into the Communion Tent and take off the four white linen vestments that he wore when he went into the Inner Sanctuary, leaving the vestments there. **16**-24 ~ He shall immerse his body in a mikvah in the sanctified area, and then put on his regular vestments. He shall then go out and complete his own ram burnt offering, thus atoning for himself and the people. **16**-25 ~ He shall also burn the choice parts of the sin offering on the altar.

**16**-26 ~ "The man who sends the Azazel goat into the desert shall immerse his clothing and body in a mikvah. Only then can he enter the camp.

**16**-27 ~ "The carcases of the bull and goat that were presented as sin offerings, whose blood was brought into the Inner Sanctuary to make atonement, shall be brought outside the camp. There, the skin, flesh and entrails shall be burned in the fire. **16**-28 ~ The one who burns them shall immerse his clothing and body in a mikvah, and he may then enter the camp.

**16**-29 ~ "All this shall be an eternal law for you. Each year, on the tenth of the seventh month, Yom Kippur, the Day of Atonement, you must fast, refrain from work, and discomfit yourselves through certain restraints. This is true of the native born and the convert who joins you. **16**-30 ~ For on this day you shall have all your sins atoned, so that you will be spiritually cleansed. You will present

*(in His nature as Source of Mercy)*

yourselves before God and He will cleanse you of all your sins. **16-31** ~ It is a Shabbat of Shabbatot to you and a day upon which you must fast. This is a law for all time.

**16-32** ~ "The priest who is anointed and installed as High Priest, from Aharon and onward, shall make this atonement, wearing the sacred vestments of white linen. **16-33** ~ He shall be the one to make atonement in the holy Inner Sanctuary, in the Communion Tent, and on the incense altar. The atonement that he makes shall be for the priests and for all the people of the community. **16-34** ~ All of this shall be for you as a law for all time in order that the Yisra'elites may gain atonement for their sins at this same time each year.

"Aharon did all this exactly as God had commanded Moshe."

**17-1** ~ God spoke to Moshe, directing him **17-2** ~ to speak to Aharon and Aharon's sons, and to the Yisra'elites, telling them these following commandments stated by God:

**17-3** ~ "If any member of the family of Yisra'el kills an ox, sheep or goat as a sacrifice to God, **17-4** ~ but does not bring it into the Communion Tent to be offered before God in His Sanctuary, that person shall be considered as if he were a murderer and he shall be cut off spiritually from among his people.

# VAYIKRA / LEVITICUS – METZORAH

*(in His nature as Source of Mercy)*

**17-5** ~ "The Yisra'elites must bring any sacrifice they are offering from the fields to the Communion Tent entrance, to give to a priest. These can then be offered as peace offerings to God.  **17-6** ~ The priest shall then dash the blood on God's altar at the entrance to the Communion Tent and burn the choice parts, creating a pleasing fragrance to God.

**17-7** ~ "The Yisra'elites must then stop sacrificing to demons or evil forces or any occult force that may tempt them, no matter where they might be nor even if it is not done for idolatry but merely to gain the favor of the force. This shall be an eternal law for all the people for all time.

**17-8** ~ "You shall also tell them that if any person, whether born of the Yisra'elites or is a convert who joins them, should he participate in any activity of a burnt offering or other sacrifice **17-9** ~ that is not brought to the Communion Tent to present it to God, that person shall be spiritually cut off from his people.

**17-10** ~ "Any person, whether he is born of the Yisra'elites or is a convert who joins them, who eats any blood of an animal, I will set My anger against that person.  **17-11** ~ Since the life-force of the flesh is in the blood and it represents the animal nature of the creature, I have given it to you to be placed on the altar to atone for your lives. For it is blood that atones for a life,  **17-12** ~ and I have instructed the Yisra'elites, as well as the converts among them, that they shall not eat blood.

# VAYIKRA / LEVITICUS – METZORAH

*(in His nature as Source of Mercy)*

**17**-13 ~ "Any person, whether he is born of the Yisra'elites or is a convert who joins them, who traps and then spills the blood of a wild animal or bird that one is permitted to eat, he must cover the blood with earth. **17**-14 ~ This is because in every living creature the blood is its life force. Tell the Yisra'elites not to eat any blood because the life force is in the blood. Whoever eats it shall be cut off spiritually from his people.

**17**-15 ~ "Any person, whether he is born of the Yisra'elites or is a convert who joins them, who eats a creature forbidden because it has a fatal lesion, or which has died on its own and not by ritual slaughter, he must immerse his clothes and his body in a mikvah, and he will remain unclean until evening. **17**-16 ~ If he does not immerse his clothes and his body in a mikvah, then when he enters the Sanctuary or when he eats any sacrifice, because his guilt has remained with him, he shall be cut off spiritually from his people."

**18**-1 ~ God spoke to Moshe, telling him to **18**-2 ~ caution the Yisra'elites, saying to them:

"I am God, Who has established the laws for your existence. **18**-3 ~ Do not follow the social ways nor the private moral relationships of the people of Egypt, where you once lived, nor of Canaan, to where I am bringing you. Do not follow the customs of those who are not of your people. **18**-4 ~ Follow My laws of social

# VAYIKRA / LEVITICUS – METZORAH

*(in His nature as Source of Mercy)*

behavior, and be careful to keep my decrees, which are necessary for the stability of the community, because I am God, your Lord. **18-5** ~ Keep my decrees and laws, for it is only by keeping them that a person can truly live. Know that I am God.

**18-6** ~ "No person shall approach a close relative for sexual purposes. Know that I am God.

**18-7** ~ "Do not commit a sexual act against your father or mother, for it is a perversion.

> **18-8** ~ "Whether your father is alive or not, do not commit incest with your father's wife, even if she is not your mother and no matter what her status is within the community.

> **18-9** ~ "Do not commit incest with your sister, even if she is only your half-sister and no matter what her status is within the community.

> **18-10** ~ "Do not commit incest with your daughter or the daughter of your son or of your daughter, for they are your own blood and this is a perversion against your own self.

# VAYIKRA / LEVITICUS – METZORAH

*(in His nature as Source of Mercy)*

**18**-11 ~ "Do not commit incest with a daughter that your father's wife has borne to your father, for she is a sister to you.

**18**-12 ~ "Do not commit incest with your father's sister, for she is in truth your blood relative.

**18**-13 ~ "Do not commit incest with your mother's sister, for she is in truth your blood relative.

**18**-14 ~ "Do not commit a sexual act with your father's brother's wife, for she is your aunt and she is forbidden to you for all time.

**18**-15 ~ "Do not commit incest with your daughter in-law, for this is an offense against your son.

**18**-16 ~ "Do not commit incest with your brother's wife, for this is an offense against your brother.

**18**-17 ~ "Do not commit incest by marrying both a woman and her daughter. It is likewise incest for you to take even her son's daughter or her daughter's daughter. They are like your blood relatives, and such an act is a perverted and sinful act.

# VAYIKRA / LEVITICUS – METZORAH

*(in His nature as Source of Mercy)*

**18**-18 ~ "Do not take the sister of your wife as another wife as long as the first one is alive, for they shall be rivals.

**18**-19 ~ "Do not come close to a woman who is in her menstrual period, or who has completed her period but has not yet immersed in a mikvah, for this is a sexual offense.

**18**-20 ~ "Do not commit a sexual act with your neighbor's wife, for she will have become defiled and forbidden to her husband.

**18**-21 ~ "Do not give in ritual any of your children to the Ammonite god Molekh, nor to any god of an idolatrous religion, for it is a profanity to God's name. This will be considered as if you had wasted the semen with which the child had been conceived. Neither shall you have intercourse with a gentile woman, for, likewise, it shall be considered as a waste of your semen. Know that I am God.

**18**-22 ~ "Do not commit a sexual-like act with a man as you would with a woman. It is considered a disgusting, perverted act.

**18**-23 ~ "Do not commit a sexual act with an animal, for it will defile you. A woman shall likewise not give herself over to an animal's sexual act. This is an utterly detestable, destructive perversion.

# VAYIKRA / LEVITICUS – METZORAH

*(in His nature as Source of Mercy)*

**18**-24 ~ "Do not let yourselves be defiled by any of these acts, as is common among the other nations. For this reason I have been driving these peoples away from before you. **18**-25 ~ They defiled their land, for which I directed my justice upon them for their sins, causing the land to violently cast out its inhabitants.

**18**-26 ~ "You, however, must keep My decrees and laws, and not become involved in any of these disgusting perversions. This is for all the Yisra'elite nation to follow, whether you are native born, a convert, or a foreigner who chooses to live among you. **18**-27 ~ The people who lived in the land before your arrival did all of these disgusting things and defiled the land.

**18**-28 ~ "Should you you defile the land, the land shall not cast you out as it did the nations that were there before you. **18**-29 ~ However, any who will do such disgusting perversions shall be cut off spiritually from his people.

**18**-30 ~ "Keep My charge to you and do not follow the perverted customs that were kept by the people before you came, so that you shall not become defiled. I am God, your Lord.

# VAYIKRA / LEVITICUS – <u>KEDOSHIM</u>
## Understanding this Holy Book

**<u>Targum Americana,</u>** as much as is possible in English, maintains the majesty of the Holy language of the Torah. It is not a translation but an interpretation, verse by verse, based on over 2,000 years of understandings offered by its original interpreters and the great later Jewish Sages and commentators.

Study of this work is not a substitute for learning Torah in the original Holy Language. Learning Torah without the clarifications of the Sages and commentators surely will lead to gross errors in understanding.

# VAYIKRA / LEVITICUS – KEDOSHIM

*(in His nature as Source of Mercy)*

**19**-1 ~ God spoke to Moshe, telling him to **19**-2 ~ speak to the entire Yisra'elite community and say to them"

"You must be holy just as I, God, Who created you, am holy.

**19**-3 ~ "Every person must regard his mother and father with reverence and with respect, and keep My Shabbatot under all circumstances. It is God, your Lord who wants this of you.

**19**-4 ~ "Do not turn aside from Me to follow false gods. Do not make yourselves gods of cast metal. It is God, your Lord who wants this of you.

**19**-5 ~ "When you offer a peace offering that is sacrificed to God, you shall do so of your own free will. **19**-6 ~ You can eat it on the day you sacrifice it and on the next day. However, you must burn in fire anything remaining from the sacrifice on the third day. **19**-7 ~ You may not even plan to eat anything from the sacrifice on the third day, for it is considered putrid and it will not be accepted as your sacrifice. **19**-8 ~ If a person does eat from the sacrifice on the third day, he has desecrated that which is holy to God and this guilt shall be upon him. This person shall be cut off spiritually from his people.

**19**-9 ~ "When you reap the harvest from your land, leave a portion

# VAYIKRA / LEVITICUS – KEDOSHIM

at the end of your field untouched. During the harvest should one or two stalks fall to the ground you must leave them on the ground. **19**-10 ~ You may not pick grapes that have not properly formed on a central stem, nor may you pick up from the ground one or two fallen grapes, but a cluster of three or more is permissible. All of these which have fallen must be left on the ground for the poor, whether a convert or a foreigner who chooses to live among you. It is God, your Lord who wants this of you.

**19**-11 ~ "Do not steal. Do not deny a rightful claim. Do not lie to one another.

**19**-12 ~ "Do not swear falsely by My name, for if you do so, you will be desecrating the name of your God. It is God, your Lord who wants this of you.

**19**-13 ~ "Do not unjustly withhold that which is due your neighbor, nor use deception to deprive him of possessions rightfully owed to him. Do not delay until the next day the wages due your worker.

**19**-14 ~ "Do not curse anyone, even the deaf.

**19**-15 ~ "Do not pervert justice. Do not give special consideration to the poor, nor show any exceptional regard to the prominent or distinguished. Judge your people fairly.

# VAYIKRA / LEVITICUS – KEDOSHIM

*(in His nature as Source of Mercy)*

**19**-16 ~ "Do not spread gossip among your people. Do not stand idly by with indifference when your neighbor's life is in danger. It is God, your Lord who wants this of you.

**19**-17 ~ "Do not hate your brother, even if it is only secretly within you. You must admonish your neighbor should he bring sin upon himself, but take care not to embarrass him in public.

**19**-18 ~ "Do not take revenge nor even continue holding ill feelings against he who has done wrong to you. You must love your neighbor as you love yourself, rejoicing in his good fortune and grieving at his misfortune. It is God, your Lord who wants this of you.

**19**-19 ~ "Keep these, My decrees:

"Do not crossbreed your livestock with other species.
"Do not plant your fields with different species of seeds.
"Do not wear a garment that contains a forbidden fabric, this being a mixture of linen and wool, whether spun together, woven together, or sewn together.

**19**-20 ~ "If a man lies carnally with a gentile woman purchased as a slave, and she has a legally recognized husband although she is not yet a completely redeemed, free person, then she has acted disgracefully and must be flogged. Because she was not yet a

# VAYIKRA / LEVITICUS – KEDOSHIM

*(in His nature as Source of Mercy)*

fully-free person, neither she nor the man shall be put to death. **19**-21 ~ But for the man's own guilt he must bring a ram as a guilt offering to God at the entrance to the Communion Tent. **19**-22 ~ For the sin that he has committed, the priest shall make atonement for him before God with the ram. He will thus gain forgiveness for his sin.

**19**-23 ~ "When you come to the land which I have promised to you, and you plant any tree which can bear edible fruit, this fruit shall be forbidden to you for the first three years after the planting; it may not be eaten nor used in any way. **19**-24 ~ The fruit of its fourth year is holy to you, for it may be eaten only in a holy place and only after you have praised God Who has provided this fruit for you. **19**-25 ~ In the fifth year you may eat its fruit or use it in any ordinary way. Thus, your produce shall increase for you from this time onward. It is God, your Lord who wants this of you.

**19**-26 ~ "Do not consume blood, nor eat of an animal before it has died, nor begin eating the flesh of a sacrificial animal before its blood has been sprinkled.

"Do not eat of an animal that has been used to seek out omens, for these are forbidden magical and superstitious acts.

**19**-27 ~ "Do not cut off completely the hair on the sides of your head. Neither shall you shave off the edges of your beard.

# VAYIKRA / LEVITICUS – KEDOSHIM

*(in His nature as Source of Mercy)*

**19**-28 ~ "Do not make gashes in your skin, such as others do as a sign of mourning. Neither shall you make tattoo marks on your skin. It is God, your Lord who wants this of you.

**19**-29 ~ "Do not accept behavior from your daughter of any debauchery or sexual relations outside of marriage, for the land will become filled with lewd sensuality and perversion.

**19**-30 ~ "Keep My Shabbatot and maintain the holy reverence of the Sanctuary where My Presence resides. It is God, your Lord who wants this of you.

**19**-31 ~ "Do not consult mediums or those who seek to contact the dead, nor oracles and diviners seeking special signs, for you defile yourselves through them. It is God, your Lord who wants this of you.

**19**-32 ~ "Stand up to respect and honor one who has lived many years, or who has acquired wisdom. In this way you shall show reverence for your God. It is God, your Lord who wants this of you.

**19**-33 ~ "When a convert comes to live in your land you shall neither do nor say anything to cause him embarrassment. **19**-34 ~ You shall accept him as if he were born of your people as you were. You shall be protective of his well-being, for you, too,

*(in His nature as Source of Mercy)*

were strangers in Egypt. It is God, your Lord who wants this of you.

**19**-35 ~ "Do not falsify measurements, neither in length, weight, or volume. **19**-36 ~ You must have an honest balance scale, honest balance weights, an honest dry measure, and an honest liquid measure.

I am God your Lord who took you out of Egypt. **19**-37 ~ Safeguard all My decrees and all My laws and keep them. It is God, your Lord who wants this of you.

**20**-1 ~ God spoke to Moshe, telling him to **20**-2 ~ say the following to the Yisra'elites:

"If any person, whether born of a Yisra'elite or who joins Yisra'el as a convert, gives any of his children to the deity Molekh, he must be put to death if a trial should find him guilty. The people shall then pelt him to death with stones. **20**-3 ~ I will direct My anger against that person and cut him off spiritually from among his people, for in giving his children to Molekh he has defiled that which is holy to Me and he has profaned My holy name. **20**-4 ~ But if the people shall ignore the fact that he gave his children to Molekh and choose not to kill him, **20**-5 ~ I will direct My anger against the transgressor and his family. He as well as all those who

*(in His nature as Source of Mercy)*

have been misled by him I will cut off spiritually from among their people for having corrupted themselves to Molekh.

**20-6** ~ "If a person turns to mediums or those who seek to contact the dead, or to oracles and diviners, seeking special signs, thereby prostituting himself to their ways, I will cut him off spiritually from among his people.

**20-7** ~ "You must sanctify yourselves and be holy, for I am God your Lord.  **20-8** ~ Safeguard My decrees and keep them, for I am God Who is making you holy by appointing you as guardians of My laws.

**20-9** ~ "Any man or woman who curses their father or mother, their step-father or step-mother, their father-in-law or mother-in-law, the community shall put that person to death by stoning.

**20-10** ~ "If a man commits adultery with a woman who is married to a Yisra'elite, both the adulterer and adulteress shall be put to death by strangulation.

**20-11** ~ "If a man has intercourse with his father's wife, this is a sexual offense against his father.  The community shall put both of them to death by stoning.

# VAYIKRA / LEVITICUS – KEDOSHIM

*(in His nature as Source of Mercy)*

**20**-12 ~ "If a man has intercourse with his daughter-in-law, this is an utterly detestable, destructive perversion. The community shall put both of them to death by stoning.

**20**-13 ~ "If a man performs a sexual act with another man in the same manner as with a woman, this is an utterly detestable, destructive perversion. The community shall put both of them to death by stoning.

**20**-14 ~ "If a man marries both a woman and her mother this is a perversion. Both he and the second of the two women he married shall be burned by fire. Such indecency shall not be tolerated among you.

**20**-15 ~ "If a man performs a sexual act with an animal, for such a degenerate act both he and the animal shall be put to death.

**20**-16 ~ "If a woman presents herself to an animal and allows it to mate with her, the community shall kill both the woman and the animal by stoning.

**20**-17 ~ "If a man takes his sister in a sexual act, and even if she is only his half-sister, it does not matter if it is by mutual consent for this is a shameful perversion. They both shall be cut off spiritually from among their people. Since he has committed incest with his sister, he shall be weighed down by his guilt until it brings him to destruction.

# VAYIKRA / LEVITICUS – KEDOSHIM

*(in His nature as Source of Mercy)*

**20**-18 ~ "If a man has intercourse with a women who is still ritually impure from her menstruation and has not yet immersed in a mikvah, he has committed a sexual offense with her. Contacting her menstrual blood in this way is sheer animal behavior. They both shall be cut off spiritually from among their people.

**20**-19 ~ "A man must not commit incest with his mother's sister or his father's sister. By committing incest with his blood relative, he shall be weighed down by his guilt until it brings him to destruction.

**20**-20 ~ "If a man has intercourse with his aunt, he has committed a sexual offense against his uncle. Both the man and the woman shall be weighed down by this guilt and will die without children.

**20**-21 ~ "If a man takes his brother's wife under conditions not allowed by the Law, both the man and the woman shall be weighed down by this guilt and will die without bearing children.

**20**-22 ~ "Safeguard all of My laws and My decrees and keep them, so that the land to which I am bringing you to settle shall not cast you out. **20**-23 ~ Do not follow the social ways nor the private moral relationships of the nation I am driving out before you, since I have been disgusted with them for their having performed all of these perversions.

## VAYIKRA / LEVITICUS – KEDOSHIM

*(in His nature as Source of Mercy)*

**20**-24 ~ "I have previously said to you, 'Take over their land that I shall bring you to, to possess this land of richness and abundance. I am God your Lord who has separated you from among all the nations. **20**-25 ~ You must in like manner separate out the pure animals and birds from the impure. Do not make yourselves disgusting through animals, birds or other creatures that I have separated out as being impure. **20**-26 ~ For as I, God, am holy, so, too, must you be holy because I have separated you out from among all the nations to be Mine.'

**20**-27 ~ "Any man or woman who is involved in the practices of mediums or those who seek to contact the dead, or to oracles and diviners shall be put to death. The community shall pelt them with stones until they are stoned to death."

# VAYIKRA / LEVITICUS – EMOR
## Understanding this Holy Book

**Targum Americana,** as much as is possible in English, maintains the majesty of the Holy language of the Torah. It is not a translation but an interpretation, verse by verse, based on over 2,000 years of understandings offered by its original interpreters and the great later Jewish Sages and commentators.

Study of this work is not a substitute for learning Torah in the original Holy Language. Learning Torah without the clarifications of the Sages and commentators surely will lead to gross errors in understanding.

# VAYIKRA / LEVITICUS – EMOR

*(in His nature as Source of Mercy)*

**21**-1 ~ God told Moshe to declare the following to Aharon's descendants, the priests:

"Let no priest defile himself by contact with the dead among his people, **21**-2 ~ except for such close blood relatives as his mother, father, son, daughter or brother. **21**-3 ~ Defilement also is permitted for his deceased virgin sister who is his father's daughter, provided she was not married at her death. **21**-4 ~ He may not defile himself for his dead wife if she was legally not permitted to him, since that makes him unfit for service. Nor may he defile himself for any corpse when there is someone else able to care for it, nor for a sage.

**21**-5 ~ "A priest shall not shave off patches of hair from his head. Neither may he shave the edges of his beard, nor make cuts in his skin such as others do as a sign of mourning.

**21**-6 ~ "Priests must be holy to their God, their Creator and Ruler, and not profane God's name. Since they present the fire offerings, these food offerings to God, who also is the Source of Mercy, they must attempt to remain holy always.

**21**-7 ~ "A priest shall not marry an immoral woman or a woman legally not permitted to him, nor may he marry a woman who has been divorced.

# VAYIKRA / LEVITICUS – EMOR

*(in His nature as Source of Mercy)*

"The entire tribe of Aharon must remain holy to God, their Creator and Ruler. **21-8** ~ You, the people Yisra'el, must strive to keep the priests holy, for they present the food offerings to God, who also is the Source of Mercy. The priest must be holy, just as I, God, Who created you, am holy, and I am calling you, the people Yisra'el, to this holy task.

**21-9** ~ "If a priest's married daughter defiles herself by committing adultery, she has at the same time defiled her father's position, and she must be burned in fire.

**21-10** ~ "These are the rules especially for the High Priest, he who has received the anointing oil upon his head and who has been inaugurated to wear the special priestly vestments:

> "He shall not go without a haircut, and he shall not allow his priestly vestments to be torn or have its stitches unraveled.

> **21-11** ~ "He shall not defile himself by coming in contact with a dead body, not even if it is his father or his mother. **21-12** ~ Should such a case occur he may not leave the sanctuary. In this way he shall not profane the sanctuary of his Creator and Ruler, for his God's anointing oil is upon him. It is I, God, who is Merciful, who has established this rule.

# VAYIKRA / LEVITICUS – EMOR

*(in His nature as Source of Mercy)*

**21**-13 ~ "He must marry a virgin. **21**-14 ~ He must not marry a widow, a divorced woman, or a profaned or immoral woman. The virgin that he marries can only come from his own people. **21**-15 ~ By observing these rule he will not profane his children because of his wife.

"He must do all this because I am God and I make him holy."

**21**-16 ~ God spoke to Moshe, telling him to **21**-17 ~ speak the following words to Aharon:

"Anyone among your descendants who has a blemish may not approach the alter to present his food offering to God. **21**-18 ~ Because of this blemish this priest may not offer his sacrifice.

"This includes one who is blind even in one eye, or lame, or who has a nose that does not look like a normal nose, or he has a nose which has an internal malformation, or he has a limb that does not look like a normal limb, or he limps, or he has a misshapen ear. **21**-19 ~ This also includes a man who has a crippled leg or hand, **21**-20 ~ or is a hunchback or is grossly fat, or who has a blemished eye or eyebrow, or who is a dwarf, or he has severe eczema or other obvious skin affliction or infection, or who has a hernia, or whose manhood is damaged.

# VAYIKRA / LEVITICUS – EMOR

*(in His nature as Source of Mercy)*

21-21 ~ "Any descendant of Aharon the priest who has a blemish may not approach the alter to present his fire offering to God. As long as he has a blemish he may not approach the alter to present this food offering to God. **21-22** ~ Still, he may eat the food offerings of his God, both from the holy of holies and from the holies, that is, he may eat of the meal offering, the sin offering, the guilt offering, and the peace offering. **21-23** ~ But if he has a blemish he may not approach the cloth partition in the sanctuary, and he may not approach the altar. He shall thus not defile any such sacrifice which is holy to Me, for I am God and I sanctify it."

21-24 ~ What he had been told Moshe passed on to Aharon and his sons and to all the Yisra'elites.

**22**-1 ~ God spoke these words to Moshe:

**22**-2 ~ "Speak to Aharon and his sons and tell them to be careful regarding the sacred offerings that the Yisra'elites consecrate to Me so that they do not desecrate My name, for I am God, who is holy.

**22**-3 ~ "Tell them that if any man among their descendants is in a spiritually unclean state when he presents the sacred offerings that the Yisra'elites consecrate to God, he shall be cut off spiritually from before Me, for I am God, who is holy.

*(in His nature as Source of Mercy)*

**22-4** ~ "Any descendant of Aharon who has a tzaraas mark, or a male discharge from his sex organ may not eat any sacred offerings until he has purified himself. The same is true of one who touches anyone defiled by the dead, who has had a seminal emission, **22-5** ~ or has touched any unclean smaller animal or creeping creature that breeds on land, or has touched a person who, himself, can defile anyone he touches.

**22-6** ~ "A person who touches any of these shall be unclean until evening, and he shall not eat any sacred offering unless he has immersed in a mikvah, **22-7** ~ Then, at sunset, he becomes ritually clean and he can then eat any portion of the sacred offerings to which he is entitled.

**22-8** ~ "A priest shall not eat any creature that has died on its own and not by ritual slaughter, neither shall he eat any creature which is forbidden only because it has a fatal lesion, since these will defile him. The priest must be holy, just as I, God, am holy,

**22-9** ~ "The priests shall thus keep my charge while they are ritually unclean by not eating sacred foods. I am God and I am making them holy, and this is a sin that can cause them to die.

**22-10** ~ "No Hebrew non-priest may eat any sacred offering reserved for the priests. Even if he resides with a priest or is hired by him, or even if the non-priest is his own Hebrew slave, that person may not eat the sacred offering.

## VAYIKRA / LEVITICUS – EMOR

*(in His nature as Source of Mercy)*

**22**-11 ~ "However, if a priest buys for money a gentile slave as his own property, then this slave may eat the sacred offering. So, too, may a gentile slave born in the priest's house eat his food.

**22**-12 ~ "When a priest's daughter marries a non-priest, she may no longer eat from the sacred offerings that are the priest's due. **22**-13 ~ However, should she become widowed or divorced and be without children she may return to her father's house with the same status she had as a girl, and she may eat her father's food. No non-priest may eat this sacred food reserved for the priests.

**22**-14 ~ "If a non-priest inadvertently eats such a sacred offering, he must return the same amount or equivalent substitute to the priest, plus an additional one-fifth. **22**-15 ~ In this way a non-priest shall not profane the sacred offerings which the Yisra'elites give as elevation-offering gifts in God's name. **22**-16 ~ Should he have eaten the sacred offering he will bear the guilt of sin, since I am God and I make these offerings holy."

**22**-17 ~ God spoke to Moshe, telling him to **22**-18 ~ speak to Aharon, to his sons, and to the Yisra'elites, saying to them:

"This is the law concerning any person, whether being of the family of Yisra'el or of the proselytes who join them, who offers any animal that is proper to be presented to God as a burnt offering to fulfill a general or a specific pledge or vow. **22**-19 ~ This

*(in His nature as Source of Mercy)*

offering will only be acceptable if it is an unblemished male taken from the cattle, sheep or goats.   **22**-20 ~ Do not present any blemished animal, since it will not be accepted as it was intended.

**22**-21 ~ "In like manner, when a person presents a peace offering of cattle or sheep to fulfill a general or a specific pledge or vow, it will only be acceptable if it is an unblemished animal.  It must not have any blemish on it.

**22**-22 ~ "Thus, you may not offer any animal that is blind, even in one eye; nor has a broken limb, foot, or tail; nor has a gash or split in an eyelid, nose or lip; nor has a gash where there is a bone; nor has a severed tongue.  Neither can the animal have warts or white extending into the iris; nor have the mange skin condition or ringworm.  You may not place such an animal on the altar as a fire offering to God.  **22**-23 ~ However, if the animal has a missing or shriveled or extra limb, or a long tail, or it limps, while it is not acceptable as a pledge on the altar, it may be offered as a gift to the sanctuary.

**22**-24 ~ "Similarly, you may not offer to God any animal whose testicles have been removed or injured in any way, whether by hand or with an instrument.  Such an act you must never do, no matter in what land you may live.

## VAYIKRA / LEVITICUS – EMOR

*(in His nature as Source of Mercy)*

**22**-25 ~ "No animal with a blemish may be offered. Even a gentile who otherwise is permitted to present a sacrifice may not present an unfit animal for such a sacred act."

**22**-26 ~ God spoke these words to Moshe:

**22**-27 ~ "When a bull, sheep or goat is born, it must remain with its mother for seven days. On the eighth day it shall become acceptable as a fire offering sacrifice to God. **22**-28 ~ It makes no difference whether it is a bull, a sheep or a goat: do not slaughter the mother and her young on the same day.

**22**-29 ~ "When you sacrifice a thanksgiving offering to God, you must do so according to the Divine laws of this Torah, for it is to be a moral and spiritually uplifting expression of thanks. **22**-30 ~ This sacrifice must be eaten on the same day, with nothing left over until the next morning. I am God and I sanctify this sacrifice.

**22**-31 ~ "Be careful concerning my commandments, and keep them, for I am God your Lord.

**22**-32 ~ "Do not desecrate My holy name. I must be sanctified and enhanced among the Yisra'elites. I am God and I am making you holy and bringing you out of Egypt to be your God. I am God your Lord."

## VAYIKRA / LEVITICUS – EMOR

*(in His nature as Source of Mercy)*

**23**-1 ~ God spoke to Moshe, telling him  **23**-2 ~ to speak these words to the Yisra'elites:

"There are special times that you must celebrate as holidays to God.  Here are my special times:

**23**-3 ~ "You may do work during the six weekdays, but the seventh day is a particularly special day of rest, a Shabbat.  It is a sacred holiday to God, when you may not do anything that is like the work that will be needed to build My sanctuary.  Wherever you may live it is God's Shabbat.

**23**-4 ~ "These are God's festivals that you must celebrate as sacred holidays at their appropriate time.  **23**-5 ~ The afternoon of the 14th day of the first month (*Nissan*) is the time that you must sacrifice God's Passover offering.  **23**-6 ~ Then, on the fifteenth of that month begins God's festival of matzot.  For seven days you shall eat matzot.  **23**-7 ~ The first day of the festival shall be a sacred holiday to you.  On this day you may not do any activity that is like the work that will be needed to build My sanctuary.  **23**-8 ~ You shall then bring sacrifices for seven days.  The seventh day is a sacred holiday when you may do no work activities, the same as you have been commanded for the first day."

**23**-9 ~ God spoke to Moshe, telling him  **23**-10 ~ to speak these words to the Yisra'elites:

# VAYIKRA / LEVITICUS – EMOR

*(in His nature as Source of Mercy)*

"When you come to the land that I am going to give you and you reap its grain harvest of wheat, barley, oats, rye, or spelt, you must bring an omer *(1/10th ephah)* of your first reaping to the priest. **23**-11 ~ You shall wave it as you have been instructed, back and forth in the four compass directions and up and down, a wave offering to God, so that your grain will be acceptable for you. The priest shall make this wave offering on the second day of the Passover holiday.

**23**-12 ~ "On the day that you make the wave offering of the omer, you shall prepare an unblemished yearling sheep as a burnt offering to God. **23**-13 ~ Its accompanying meal offering shall be two-tenths of an ephah of wheat meal, mixed with oil, as a fire offering to God. Together with this is the libation offering, which shall be one-fourth hin *(about a quart)* of wine.

**23**-14 ~ "Until the day that you bring this set of sacrifices to your God, you may not eat of this harvest any bread, toasted grain, or fresh grain. This shall be an eternal law wherever you may live within the land that I am going to give you. It will be meritorious for you to observe this law even should you be living in other lands, and whether it is grain grown by Yisra'elites or by those from the other nations.

**23**-15 ~ "Beginning on the day when you have brought the omer as a wave offering, you shall count seven complete weeks,

*(in His nature as Source of Mercy)*

**23**-16 ~ until the day after the seventh week, when you will have counted 50 days. On this 50th day you may present two loaves of this new grain as a meal offering to God.

**23**-17 ~ "From this land which I shall be giving you, you shall bring two loaves of bread as a wave offering. They shall be made of two-tenths of an ephah of wheat flour, and shall be baked as rectangular loaves of leavened bread. They are the first-harvest offering to God.

**23**-18 ~ "Together with this bread, you shall sacrifice the following unblemished animals: one seven year-old sheep, one young bull, and two rams. These sacrifices and the meal offering and libations shall be a burnt offering to God, a fire offering as an appeasing fragrance to God.

**23**-19 ~ "You shall also prepare one goat as a sin offering, and two year-old sheep as peace sacrifices. **23**-20 ~ The priest shall make the prescribed wave motions for a wave offering before God, along with the bread for the first-harvest offering and the two sheep. These are sacred to God, and they shall belong to the priest.

**23**-21 ~ "This very day shall be celebrated as a sacred holiday, when you may not do any activity that is like the work that will be needed to build My sanctuary. This shall be an eternal law for all time wherever you may live within the land that I am going to give you.

## VAYIKRA / LEVITICUS – EMOR

*(in His nature as Source of Mercy)*

**23**-22 ~ "Furthermore, when you reap your land's harvest, do not completely harvest to the ends of your fields. Should individual stalks fall do not pick them up. These must be left for the poor and the stranger. I am God your Lord, the Merciful God."

**23**-23 ~ God spoke to Moshe, telling him to **23**-24 ~ speak the following words to the Yisra'elites"

"The first day of the seventh month *(Tishrei)* shall be a day of rest. It is a sacred holiday of remembrance and gratitude to God for His gift of freedom and prosperity, and the ram's horn shall be sounded on this day. **23**-25 ~ It is a day when you may not take any action that is like the work that will be needed to build My sanctuary. On this day you must bring a fire offering to God."

**23**-26 ~ God spoke these words to Moshe:

**23**-27 ~ "The 10<sup>th</sup> of this seventh month shall be your Day of Atonement *(Yom Kippur)*. It is a sacred holiday when you must fast, refrain from work, and discomfit yourselves through certain restraints. On this day you must bring a fire offering to God. **23**-28 ~ Do not do any work on this day, as you would not do on the Shabbat, not even preparing food. It is a day for making amends before God, for you to gain atonement before Him.

## VAYIKRA / LEVITICUS – EMOR

*(in His nature as Source of Mercy)*

**23**-29 ~ "If anyone does not fast on this day, he shall be cut off spiritually from his people.

**23**-30 ~ "Similarly, if one does any forbidden work on this day, he thus denies that his life is responsible to God, and I will utterly destroy him spiritually from his people.

**23**-31 ~ "Do not do any forbidden work on this day. This is an eternal law for all generations wherever you may live. **23**-32 ~ It is a Shabbat of Shabbatot, a particularly holy day, when you must fast. You must keep this day holy from the ninth of the month until the next night."

**23**-33 ~ God spoke to Moshe, telling him to **23**-34 ~ speak the following words to the Yisra'elites:

"The fifteenth of the seventh month shall begin the festival of Sukkot to God, which shall last for seven days. **23**-35 ~ The first day shall be a sacred holiday. Do not do any work on this day, as you would not do on the Shabbat. **23**-36 ~ On each of these seven days you shall bring a fire offering to God.

"The eighth day is likewise a sacred holiday to you, for on it you shall bring a fire offering to God. It is a holy time, when you may not do any work on this day, just as you would not do on the Shabbat.

# VAYIKRA / LEVITICUS – EMOR

*(in His nature as Source of Mercy)*

**23**-37 ~ "All of these holy days are God's special times which you must keep as sacred holidays. They are times when you must present to God a burnt offering, a meal offering, a sacrifice and libations, each according to its special day. **23**-38 ~ This is in addition to the Shabbat offerings, and the gifts and the specific and general pledges that you offer to God.

**23**-39 ~ "On the fifteenth of the seventh month, when you harvest the land's grain, you shall celebrate a festival to God for seven days. The first day shall be a day of rest, like the Shabbat, and the eighth day also shall be a day of rest.

**23**-40 ~ "On the first day of the festival of Sukkot you must take for yourself a fruit of the citron tree *(an etrog)*, an unopened palm frond, three myrtle branches, and two willow twigs from the trees that grow near streams. You shall rejoice before God for seven days. **23**-41 ~ Each year, during these seven days you shall celebrate to God. This shall be an eternal law for all time wherever you may live that you celebrate this festival in the seventh month.

**23**-42 ~ "During these seven days all Yisra'elites must live in temporary huts *(sukkot)* covered with thatched roofs. **23**-43 ~ In this way all future generations will know that when I brought them out of Egypt, while they were in the desert I had them live in these temporary dwellings, surrounded by the clouds of glory. I am God your Lord, the Merciful God."

# VAYIKRA / LEVITICUS – EMOR

*(in His nature as Source of Mercy)*

**23**-44 ~ "Moshe related all of these rules of God's special times to the Yisra'elites.

**24**-1 ~ God spoke to Moshe these words:

> **24**-2 ~ "Instruct the Yisra'elites to bring you clear illuminating oil from olives hand-crushed in a mortar, to keep the lamp continually burning.

> **24**-3 ~ "Aharon shall light the lamp only with this oil. It shall burn before God outside the cloth partition in the Communion Tent from evening until morning, This shall be an eternal law for all time. **24**-4 ~ Before God, he shall light the lamps on the pure gold menorah only with this oil.

> **24**-5 ~ "You shall take the finest grade of wheat flour and bake it into twelve loaves. Each loaf shall contain two-tenths of an ephah *(about one gallon)*. **24**-6 ~ Arrange these loaves in two stacks, six loaves to each stack. This shall be placed on the undefiled acacia wood table which is before God.

> **24**-7~ "Place a bowl containing pure frankincense alongside these stacks. This will be the memorial portion presented as a fire offering to God.

# VAYIKRA / LEVITICUS – EMOR

*(in His nature as Source of Mercy)*

**24-8**~ "These loaves shall be arranged before God each Shabbat. It is an eternal decree, a covenant with the Yisra'elites.  **24-9**~ The bread shall be given to Aharon and his descendants, but since it is holy of holies among God's fire offerings, they must eat it in a sanctified area. This bread is their due for all time."

**24-10** ~ The son of a Yisra'elite woman and an Egyptian man who some time earlier had been killed by Moshe for beating a Yisra'elite working in the field, went out walking among the Yisra'elites, and he entered a quarrel with a Yisra'elite man in the camp about joining the Danite encampment  **24-11** ~ because his mother, Shelomit, was the daughter of Divri of the tribe of Dan. This son then called out the name of God and blasphemed His name with a curse. The people took him and brought him to Moshe.  **24-12** ~ They kept him under custody until the penalty could be specified by God.

**24-13** ~ God spoke the following ruling to Moshe:

**24-14** ~ "Take the blasphemer out of the camp, and let all who heard him place their hands upon his head. The entire community shall then stone him to death."

**24-15** ~ God then instructed Moshe to speak these words to the Yisra'elites: "Anyone who curses God shall bear his sin.  **24-16** ~ But if one actually blasphemes the four letter name of God, the

*(in His nature as Source of Mercy)*

Tetragrammaton YHVH, he shall be put to death. The entire community shall stone him to death. Whether he is a foreigner living in the land or a native born Yisra'elite, he shall be put to death.

**24**-17 ~ "One who takes a human life must be put to death.

**24**-18 ~ "If one kills an animal he must pay the value of that life which he has taken, the value of a life for a life.

**24**-19 ~ "If one maims his neighbor, a fitting penalty shall be established and done to him. **24**-20 ~ Thus, full compensation must be paid for a fracture or the loss of an eye or a tooth. If one inflicts injury on another person, he must pay an amount equal to what he would incur in order to avoid such injury to himself.

**24**-21 ~ "In summary then, if one kills an animal he must pay for it, but if one kills a human being, he must be put to death. **24**-22 ~ There shall be but a single law for both you as a native born Yisra'elite and for a proselyte, for I am God, Lord of all of you alike."

**24**-23 ~ Moshe related all of this to the Yisra'elites, and they took the blasphemer out of the camp and pelted him to death with stones. The Yisra'elites thus did all that God had commanded them through Moshe.

## VAYIKRA / LEVITICUS – <u>BEHAR</u>
### Understanding this Holy Book

**Targum Americana,** as much as is possible in English, maintains the majesty of the Holy language of the Torah. It is not a translation but an interpretation, verse by verse, based on over 2,000 years of understandings offered by its original interpreters and the great later Jewish Sages and commentators.


Study of this work is not a substitute for learning Torah in the original Holy Language. Learning Torah without the clarifications of the Sages and commentators surely will lead to gross errors in understanding.

# VAYIKRA / LEVITICUS – BEHAR

*(in His nature as Source of Mercy)*

**25**-1 ~ When the Yira'elites reached Mount Sinai, God spoke to Moshe, **25**-2 ~ telling him to say these words to them:

"When you come to the land that I am giving to you, the land must be given a rest period, a Shabbat to God. **25**-3 ~ For six years you may plant your fields, prune your vineyards, and harvest your crops. **25**-4 ~ When the seventh year arrives it must be a Shabbat of Shabbatot for the land. It is God's Shabbat during which you may not plant your fields nor prune your vineyards. **25**-5 ~ Do not harvest crops that may grow on their own in this year and do not gather the grapes on your unworked, unpruned vines, since it is a year of rest for the land.

**25**-6 ~ "What grows while the land is resting may be eaten by any person: you, your male and female slaves, as well as the employees and resident work force who live with you. **25**-7 ~ Any of these crops also may be eaten by domestic and wild animals that are in your land.

**25**-8 ~ "You shall count seven cycles of seven years, these seven Sabbatical cycles that add up to forty-nine years. **25**-9 ~ Then, on the 10th day of the seventh month *(Tishrei)*, you shall make a proclamation with the ram's horn. It is on this Yom Kippur day that the ram's horn proclamation shall be made, **25**-10 ~ and you shall sanctify the fiftieth year for as long as Yisra'elites are living in the land that I give you. By this you shall declare the emancipation of all your slaves, thereby restoring their dignity. This is your yovel *(jubilee)* year, when each man shall return to his hereditary property and to his family.

# VAYIKRA / VAYIKRA / LEVITICUS – BEHAR

*(in His nature as Source of Mercy)*

**25**-11 ~ "Like the forty-ninth year, the fiftieth year also shall be God's Shabbat year for you, when you shall not harvest crops that may grow on their own in this year and not gather the grapes on your unworked, unpruned vines, since it is a year of rest for the land. **25**-12 ~ The yovel, when the land is resting, shall be holy to you, for what may be picked and eaten is only what you need of what grows on its own.

**25**-13 ~ "In the yovel year, every man shall return to his hereditary property. **25**-14 ~ Thus, when you buy or sell land to your neighbor, do not cheat one another. **25**-15 ~ If you are a buyer, you are buying only according to the number of years since the previous yovel. The seller is only selling to you for the number of years the land will produce crops until the next yovel. **25**-16 ~ The more years remaining, the higher the price shall be. **25**-17 ~ You will then not be taking advantage of one another. You shall respect the feelings of one another. I am present at all your transactions, therefore fear Me, God, your Lord.

**25**-18 ~ "Keep My decrees and safeguard My laws. If you keep them you will live securely in the land. **25**-19 ~ The land will produce its fruit, and you will eat your fill, thus living securely in the land.

**25**-20 ~ "As the yovel year approaches, you may ask, 'What shall we eat in the yovel year? We have not planned nor have we harvested crops.'

**25**-21 ~ "I will direct my blessing to you in the sixth year, and the land will produce enough crops for three years. **25**-22 ~ There will be

# VAYIKRA / VAYIKRA / LEVITICUS – BEHAR

*(in His nature as Source of Mercy)*

sufficient harvest so that you will have enough of the old crop to eat while you are planting after the eighth year, and on into the ninth year until your crops have ripened.

**25-23** ~ "Since the land is Mine, no land may be sold permanently.  As I look upon you, you are all foreigners and resident aliens.  **25-24** ~ Therefore, there shall be a time for redemption of all your hereditary lands.

**25-25** ~ "If your fellow Yisra'elite becomes impoverished and sells some of his hereditary land, a close relative can redeem what was sold after two years have passed.  The buyer can not challenge this redemption.  **25-26** ~ Should the seller have no one to redeem that land for him, then if he should acquire enough wealth he may redeem the land himself, the same as a kinsman could have redeemed it for him.  **25-27** ~ The redemption shall be calculated according to how many years are left until the next yovel, and he shall return the balance to the buyer.  He can then return to his hereditary land.

**25-28** ~ "If he does not have the means to redeem the land, the land shall remain with the buyer until the yovel year,  It shall then be released and returned to the original owner.

**25-29** ~ "When a man sells a residence house in a walled city *(these being the walled cities at the time Joshua conquered the land)*, he shall be able to redeem it until the end of one year from the time he sold it.  This is

*(in His nature as Source of Mercy)*

exactly one year to the day. **25-30** ~ If the time to redeem the property has passed, then that house in the walled city shall become the permanent possession of the buyer, able to be passed down to his descendants. The yovel year shall not force its return to the seller.

**25-31** ~ "On the other hand, houses in villages without walls around them shall be considered the same as open land. They can be redeemed, and the yovel year does force its return to the seller.

**25-32** ~ "As for the cities of the Levites, the Levites shall always have the power to redeem the houses in their hereditary cities. **25-33** ~ Thus, if one buys a house or city from the Levites, it must be released by the yovel, for the Levite cities are their permanent hereditary property among the Yisra'elites. **25-34** ~ Similarly, the 3,000 cubits of open area around their cities may not be sold as a permanent possession of the buyer because it is their hereditary property forever.

**25-35** ~ "If your fellow Yisra'elite becomes impoverished and loses his ability to support himself in the community, you must come to his aid. Help him to survive in whatever way he may need, whether he is a proselyte or native born Yisra'elite.

**25-36** ~ "Do not take advanced interest or accrued interest from him for a loan. Fear your God, and let your fellow Yisra'elite live alongside you. **25-37** ~ Do not make him pay advanced interest for your money, and do not give him food for which he will have to pay accrued

*(in His nature as Source of Mercy)*

interest.  **25**-38 ~ Do this, for I am God who brought you out of Egypt to give you the land of Canaan, and to be your God.

**25**-39 ~ "If your fellow Yisra'elite becomes impoverished and is sold to you because of his poverty, do not work him like a slave.  **25**-40 ~ He shall be treated by you no differently than if he were an employee or a resident worker.  He shall serve you only until the yovel year,  **25**-41 ~ at which time he and his children shall be free to leave you and return to their family.  He shall thus return to the hereditary land of his ancestors.  **25**-42 ~ This is because I brought the Yisra'elites out of the land of Egypt, and they are My servants.  They shall not be sold in any manner as slaves.  **25**-43 ~ Do not treat this person in any way that may break his spirit, for in this shall you feel the fear of your God.

**25**-44 ~ "You may have slaves who are not Yisra'elites, males or females, purchased from the nations around you.  **25**-45 ~ You can also purchase such slaves from the resident aliens who live among you, and from their families born in your land.  All are your hereditary property  **25**-46 ~ that you may pass down to your children.  You shall thus have them serve you forever.

"However, your fellow Yisra'elites you must not treat in this way.  They are your brethren, and you must not treat them in any way that may break their spirit.

# VAYIKRA / VAYIKRA / LEVITICUS – BEHAR

*(in His nature as Source of Mercy)*

**25**-47 ~ "This is the law if a foreigner or resident alien gains favorable position over your brother who has lost his means of support and is sold to a foreigner, a resident alien, an apostate, or to an idolatrous cult or family.

**25**-48 ~ "After he has been sold into slavery, he must be redeemed, preferably, by a close relative who has the means. **25**-49 ~ This includes his uncle or cousin, or any other close relative. The closest capable relative may not refuse to redeem him. If he obtains the means, even through borrowing, he can redeem himself.

**25**-50 ~ "In all such cases, the redemption shall be calculated according to how many years are left until the next yovel. The purchase price shall be agreed upon between the redeemer and the one who bought him for the number of years as if he were hired for that amount.

**25**-51 ~ "If many years are left until the yovel the redemption money shall be greater than **25**-52 ~ the amount returned if fewer years are left until the yovel. They shall settle upon the redemption money according to the number of years he has already worked.

**25**-53 ~ "Such a slave shall be considered as if he were an employee hired on a yearly basis. If you become aware that his master has been treating him in any way that could break his spirit, you may not remain quiet about this.

**25**-54 ~ "If the slave is not redeemed by any of these means, he and his children shall be freed in the yovel year.

# VAYIKRA / VAYIKRA / LEVITICUS – BEHAR

*(in His nature as Source of Mercy)*

**25**-54 ~ "All of this that I have instructed you is because I brought the Yisra'elites out of the land of Egypt, and they are My servants. I am God, Lord of all of you alike.

**26**-1 ~ "Therefore, do not make for yourselves false gods. Do not establish a stone idol or a sacred pillar for yourselves. Do not place a stone in your land for veneration or contemplation or for kneeling or prostrating yourselves to any deity, not even to Me. Only I am God, and this is my instruction to you.

**26**-2 ~ "Keep my Shabbatot and revere My sanctuary. Only I am God, and this is my instruction to you.

## VAYIKRA / LEVITICUS – <u>BECHUKOTAI</u>
## Understanding this Holy Book

**<u>Targum Americana,</u>** as much as is possible in English, maintains the majesty of the Holy language of the Torah. It is not a translation but an interpretation, verse by verse, based on over 2,000 years of understandings offered by its original interpreters and the great later Jewish Sages and commentators.

Study of this work is not a substitute for learning Torah in the original Holy Language. Learning Torah without the clarifications of the Sages and commentators surely will lead to gross errors in understanding.

# VAYIKRA / LEVITICUS – BECHUKOTAI

*(in His nature as Source of Mercy)*

**26**-3 ~ "If you follow my laws and are careful to keep My commandments, **26**-4 ~ I will provide you with rain at the right time, so that the land will bear its crops and the trees of the field will provide their fruit. **26**-5 ~ These will produce so much that your threshing season will last until your grape harvest, and your grape harvest will last until the time you plant your fields. You will have your fill of food and you will live securely in the land.

**26**-6 ~ "I will grant peace in the land so that you will sleep without fear. I will rid the land of dangerous animals, and the sword of war will not pass through your land. **26**-7 ~ You will chase away your enemies, for they will lose their courage and fall before your might. **26**-8 ~ Five of you will be able to chase away one hundred, and one hundred of you will defeat ten thousand, as your enemies fall before you.

**26**-9 ~ "I will turn to you with favor, making you fertile and numerous, for I keep my covenant with you.

**26**-10 ~ "The previous year's crop will be more than sufficient to feed you in this year, and so much will remain that you will have to clear out the old to make room for the new harvest.

**26**-11 ~ "I will keep My sanctuary in your midst, neither shall I reject you as My chosen nation. **26**-12 ~ I will make My presence felt among you. Thus, I will be your God, and you will be a nation dedicated to Me.

# VAYIKRA / LEVITICUS – BECHUKOTAI

*(in His nature as Source of Mercy)*

**26**-13 ~ "I am God, your Lord. I brought you out to freedom from Egypt, where you were slaves. I broke the restraints binding you to their oppression, and I led you out with your heads held high.

**26**-14 ~ "If you do not listen to me and you do not keep all of My commandments, **26**-15 ~ if you denigrate My decrees and grow tired of My laws, then you will have broken My covenant with you. **26**-16 ~ I will then do the same to you. I will bring upon you feelings of anxiety, trembling, and terror, along with depression, fever, and various diseases within your body and on your skin. You will have little to look forward to and you will feel that your life is hopeless.

"You will plant your crop in vain because not you but your enemies will eat it. **26**-17 ~ I will direct My anger against you, so that your enemies will defeat you and dominate you. You will flee even when no one is chasing you.

**26**-18 ~ "If you persist in not listening to Me, I will increase the punishments for your sins seven fold. **26**-19 ~ I will break your haughtiness and aggressive behavior toward Me. Your skies will be as impenetrable as iron to you and not able to provide its favor to you. **26**-20 ~ Your efforts will exhaust you to no avail, for your land will be as hard as brass and not able to provide its yield for you, nor will the trees produce their fruit for you.

**26**-21 ~ "If you become indifferent to Me, giving Me little of your concern

# VAYIKRA / LEVITICUS – BECHUKOTAI

*(in His nature as Source of Mercy)*

and you no longer desire to obey me, or if you act as if I am a burden to you, then as you act towards Me so shall I act towards you, and I will again increase the punishments for your sins seven fold. **26**-22 ~ I will send wild beasts among you, killing your children, destroying your livestock, and reducing your numbers so that your roads will become empty of you.

**26**-23 ~ "If all this is not yet enough to have you change your ways, and you remain indifferent or antagonistic towards Me, **26**-24 ~ then I will be likewise towards you, and I will yet again increase the punishments for your sins seven fold. **26**-25 ~ I will bring an unrelenting sword against you to protect My covenant of Justice, Morality and Humanity with the nations, whom you will have joined in degeneration, and you will thereby huddle in fear in your cities. Moreover, I will send the plague against you, and give you into the hand of your enemies.

**26**-26 ~ "I will cut off your food supply and take away what nourishment is contained in the remaining food you do have. You will have so little grain and fuel that ten women will be able to bake bread in one oven, and what they bring back to their families will not be enough to satisfy their hunger, nor provide enough nourishment.

**26**-27 ~ "If you still do not obey me and remain indifferent to Me, **26**-28 ~ My indifference to you, in turn, will be with a vengeance, and I will once again increase your punishments seven fold because of your

*(in His nature as Source of Mercy)*

rebellion against Me. **26**-29 ~ So intense will your hunger be that you will eat the flesh of your own sons and daughters. **26**-30 ~ When I destroy your towers and altars toward which you direct your worship, and smash your idolatrous statues and images, I will allow your corpses to rot on their remains.

"I will thus have grown tired of your behavior, and I will sever the living relationship between you and Me. **26**-31 ~ I will let your cities fall into ruins and make your sanctuaries desolate. No longer will I accept the pleasing fragrance of your sacrifices. **26**-32 ~ I will make the land so desolate that your enemies who live there will be unable to restore it to the prosperity that I had previously conferred upon it. **26**-33 ~ I will scatter you among the nations, and your fear of them and their enmity towards you shall follow you. Your land will remain bleak and inhospitable and so, too, your broken cities.

**26**-34 ~ "In this way, while you will be in the land of your enemies, your land will remain desolate in order to regain its lost Shabbatot; the land will rest and enjoy its Sabbatical years. **26**-35 ~ So long as the land remains desolate, the land shall keep the Shabbat, which you did not allow it while you lived there.

**26**-36 ~ "Those of you who will survive in the land of your enemies will feel as insecure as when you were slaves in Egypt. The sound of rustling leaves will panic you as if the sword were coming after you. Though none will be chasing you, **26**-37 ~ such fear will cause you to fall over

# VAYIKRA / LEVITICUS – BECHUKOTAI

*(in His nature as Source of Mercy)*

one another in your haste to flee from this imagined enemy. There will be none among you willing to stand up to your illusory foe.

**26-38** ~ "The land of your enemies will consume you and you will thus be destroyed from among the nations.

**26-39** ~ "The few of you who then remain alive in the land of your enemies will finally realize that your survival is threatened because you have not kept My decrees and safeguarded My laws, neither you nor your fathers. **26-40** ~ You will then confess your sins and the sins of your fathers for your transgressions and for being false to Me. **26-41** ~ It is for this that I have been indifferent to your fathers and have them brought into the land of their enemies, where the remaining few will survive.

"When this time finally comes that their stubborn spirit becomes humbled, I will forgive their sin. **26-42** ~ I will remember My covenant with Yaakov as well as My covenant with Yitzchak and My covenant with Avraham. And I will remember, too, the land. **26-43** ~ For the land will have been left behind by them, and will have enjoyed its Shabbatot while it lay in desolation without them. And, so, the sin they had committed by denigrating My laws and growing tired of My decrees will become remedied.

**26-44** ~ "Thus, even when they are in their enemies' land, I will not grow so disgusted with them nor so tired of them and their behaviors that I would destroy them and break My covenant with them, since I am and

# VAYIKRA / LEVITICUS – BECHUKOTAI

*(in His nature as Source of Mercy)*

remain God, their Lord. **26**-45 ~ I will therefore remember the covenant with their ancestors whom I brought out of the land of Egypt in the sight of the nations, becoming a God to them, and so I remain."

**26**-46 ~ These are the decrees, laws, and codes that God set between Himself and the Yisra'elites through the hand of Moshe at Mount Sinai.

**27**-1 ~ God spoke to Moshe, **27**-2 ~ telling him to relate the following to the Yisra'elites:

"This is the law when a person makes a vow *(neder)* to donate to God the monetary value of a person.

> **27**-3 ~ "The valuation for a male from 20 to 60 years of age is 50 shekels in silver *(based on the sanctuary standard of eight-tenths of an ounce of silver per shekel)*. **27**-4 ~ For a woman this shall be 30 shekels. **27**-5 ~ For a male from 5 to 20 years of age the valuation is 20 shekels in silver, but for a woman this shall be 10 shekels. **27**-6 ~ For a male from 1 month to 5 years of age the valuation is 5 shekels in silver, but for a female this shall be 3 shekels. **27**-7 ~ For a man over 60 years of age the valuation is 15 shekels in silver, and 10 shekels for a woman.

**27**-8 ~ "If a person is too poor to pay the endowment, he shall come before the priest so that the priest can determine what the endowment

# VAYIKRA / LEVITICUS – BECHUKOTAI

*(in His nature as Source of Mercy)*

value shall be. The priest shall make his determination on the basis of how much the person making the vow can afford.

27-9 ~ "This is the law when a person makes a vow *(neder)* to sacrifice to God a proper animal, then it automatically becomes consecrated at that moment. 27-10 ~ The animal may neither be exchanged for another kind nor may a substitute of the same kind be offered in its place. It does not matter whether one of these animals is a better or a worse animal. If a replacement does occur, both the original animal and the replacement shall be consecrated.

27-11 ~ "If the animal that was offered happens to be unfit for sacrifice to God because of a blemish, the owner shall bring the animal to the priest. 27-12 ~ The priest shall sct the endowment value according to the animal's good and bad qualities and its usefulness for the House of God. The animal's endowment value shall be whatever the priest determines. 27-13 ~ If the owner wishes to redeem the animal, he must add 20% to its endowment value.

27-14 ~ "If a person consecrates his house as something sacred to God, the priest shall set the endowment value according to its good and bad qualities. The endowment value shall be whatever the priest determines. 27-15 ~ If the owner wishes to redeem the house, he must add 20% to its endowment value and the house then reverts back to him.

# VAYIKRA / LEVITICUS – BECHUKOTAI

*(in His nature as Source of Mercy)*

27-16 ~ "If a man consecrates to God a field from his hereditary property, its endowment shall be calculated according to the amount of seed required to sow it, 50 shekels for each chomer of barley seed *(about 220 liters, or enough seed to cover 75,000 square cubits)*. 27-17 ~ This is the endowment valuation that must be paid just after the yovel year. 27-18 ~ However, if one consecrates his field in a later year, the priest shall calculate the endowment value and then reduce it according to how many years remain until the next yovel year.

27-19 ~ "If the person wishes to redeem the field, he must add 20% to its endowment value and the field then reverts back to him. 27-20 ~ Should he not redeem the field, or if the Sanctuary Treasurer immediately sells the field to another person, it can no longer be redeemed. 27-21 ~ When the next yovel year comes, the field is then released and becomes consecrated to God, just like a field that has been vowed as hallowed. It then becomes the hereditary property of the priest on duty at the start of the yovel year.

27-22 ~ "If the consecrated field is not the person's hereditary possession but a field that he has bought, 27-23 ~ the priest shall calculate the endowment valuation and then reduce it according to how many years remain until the next yovel year. On that day of endowment anyone can redeem it by giving its endowment valuation to the priest as something consecrated to God. 27-24 ~ In any case, when the yovel year arrives the field shall revert to the one from whom it had been bought, returning to him his hereditary property.

## VAYIKRA / LEVITICUS – BECHUKOTAI

*(in His nature as Source of Mercy)*

**27-25** ~ "Every endowment valuation shall be according to the Sanctuary standard, where the shekel is 20 gerahs *(about 0.8 ounces)*.

**27-26** ~ "An animal which is a first-born and must be offered as a sacrifice to God may not be consecrated or assigned for any other purpose. Whether it is an ox, a sheep, or a goat, it automatically belongs to God.

**27-27** ~ "If a non-kosher animal is consecrated, it may be redeemed for its endowment valuation plus 20%. If it is not redeemed it shall be sold for its endowment value.

**27-28** ~ "Anything hallowed to God, whether done so for the Temple or for the priests, whether it already was hallowed or it is now being hallowed, can not be sold or redeemed. This is true for anything he owns, whether it is a slave, an animal, or a hereditary field. Everything that is hallowed is holy of holies to God. **27-29** ~ If a human being is declared hallowed by the King or the Sanhedrin, he can not be redeemed and must be put to death.

**27-30** ~ "The tithes of the land *(maaser sheni)*, whether of the crops of the soil or the fruit of the trees, are consecrated to God and belong to Him. **27-31** ~ If a person wishes to redeem such tithes, he must add an additional 20%.

**27-32** ~ "All tithes of the herds and flocks shall be given when they are counted under the rod, with every tenth animal being consecrated to God.

## VAYIKRA / LEVITICUS – BECHUKOTAI

*(in His nature as Source of Mercy)*

**27**-33 ~ No distinction shall be made between better and worse animals, and no substitutions are permitted. If a substitution actually is made, then both the original animal and the replacement shall be consecrated, and neither one may be redeemed."

**27**-34 ~ "These are the commandments that God gave Moshe for the Yisra'elites at Mount Sinai.

**CHAZAK**

# TRANSLITERATIONS

| THIS TARGUM | THE VERNACULAR | THIS TARGUM | THE VERNACULAR |
|---|---|---|---|
| Aharon | *Aaron* | Noach | *Noah* |
| Avram | *Abram* | Plishtim | *Philistines* |
| Avraham | *Abraham* | Reuven | *Reuben* |
| Bavel | *Babylon* | Rivka | *Rebecca* |
| Bet El | *Bethel* | Shabbat / Shabbatot | *Sabbath – Shabbos / Sabbaths* |
| Bet Lechem | *Bethlehem* | Shaul | *Saul* |
| Binyamin | *Benjamin* | Shavuot | *Shavuoth / Shavuos* |
| Cham | *Ham* | Shim'on | *Simeon* |
| Chanoch | *Enoch* | Tzaraas | *Leprosy (incorrect translation)* |
| Chava | *Eve* | Tzidon | *Sidon* |
| Cheth | *Heth* | Yaakov | *Jacob* |
| Chevron | *Hebron* | Yarden | *Jordan River* |
| Dudaim | *Mandrakes* | Yehoshua | *Joshua* |
| D'vorah | *Deborah* | Yehudah | *Judah* |
| Esav | *Esau* | Yehudit | *Judith* |
| Etrog | *Esrog* | Yerushalaim | *Jerusalem* |
| Havel | *Abel* | Yishmael | *Ishmael* |
| Iyov | *Job* | Yissachar | *Issachar* |
| Yehoshua | *Joshua* | Yisra'el | *Israel* |
| Lavan | *Laban* | Yitro | *Jethro* |
| Matzot | *Matzahs* | Yitzchak | *Isaac* |
| Meheitaval | *Mehetabal* | Yosef | *Joseph* |
| Menasheh | *Manasseh* | Zevulun | *Zebulun* |
| Moshe | *Moses* | | |

**BOOKS BY Irwin Tyler (Yirmi Tyler)**

<u>SO MANY GATES TO THE CITY... A GUIDE FOR THE MODERN PERPLEXED</u>
**A Book About Jewish Belief and Understanding, and Making Some Sense Of It**

<u>TARGUM AMERICANA - BERESHIT / GENESIS</u>

<u>TARGUM AMERICANA THE BIBLE UNDERSTOOD - SHEMOT / EXODUS</u>

<u>TARGUM AMERICANA THE BIBLE UNDERSTOOD - BEMIDBAR / NUMBERS</u>

<u>COLLECTING PAPER MONEY WITH CONFIDENCE</u>

<u>GRADING COINS WITH CONFIDENCE</u>

ALL ARE AVAILABLE AT:
<u>AMAZON.COM</u>

SELECTED TITLES AVAILABLE AT:
<u>LULU.COM</u>
<u>CREATESPACE.COM</u>
<u>AHL KAYN PUBLICATIONS WEB SITE</u>